TOUCH

A Novel

by

Angela Cairns

Cover Design; Fiona Mycroft, Propaw Design

ACKNOWLEDGEMENTS

Thank you to Petra McQueen and my amazing 'Friday Friends' in the Novel Writer's Workshop at The Writers Company; Angela, Claire, Bryan, Lyndall, Sarah and Frederike – for your generous teaching, constructive feedback, patience and enthusiasm. For absolutely believing I could do this. I couldn't wish for a more nurturing environment in which to write.

Thanks to Nina Fotara for help with the website, Janette Brindle, Angela Eyre and Janis Spillett for reading the draft copy. For all your unfailing friendship and support. Particularly, for not laughing when I said what I was going to do...

To Fiona at ProPaws design, many thanks for the cover design and sorry for all the late messages.

To the Admin. team; Julie, Nadine, Louise, Miriam, the Physio team; Melanie, Reah, Adia and Dave and the amazing patients in my own clinic- you are a daily inspiration.

To my Setter and Pointer friends, Tilly and Richard, Tracy and Dave, Fran, Clare and Jeff, Karen, Trevor and so many more for sharing the crazy, wonderful world of owning a Setter and many hours (not always sunny and warm) training and working with them.

Finally, a heartfelt thank you to Phil, my husband for letting me hijack our free time to write and for remaining calm throughout the ups and downs.

DEDICATION

For Phil, Jamie and Kyle

TABLE OF CONTENTS

1. After he died

I ran down the stairs at Mum and Dad's optimistic and excited, on my way to have photos taken for my Australian visa. I picked up the phone on my way through the hall. I was initially delighted to hear my Sydney flatmate Annie's voice, until I realised she was crying.

"Annie what on earth is it?"

"Ellie, oh Ellie I don't know how to tell you... He's gone."

"Annie, who's gone? What's happened? Has something happened to Max?"

"No Ellie not Max," her voice, now a broken whisper, “Brett - there's been an accident, his plane went down this morning, Ellie, he died."

I looked at the receiver stupidly and time seemed to telescope into a long still moment where I couldn't react or feel anything and the world stopped. Then in a sudden rush, time hurtled back into the vacuum, nearly knocking me off my feet and bringing with it a cacophony of intense sensation.

The incongruous merry tinkle of an ice cream van sounded outside.

Annic’s voice, “Ellie, Ellie are you still there?”

The pattern on the wallpaper in the hall swirled and distorted in front of my eyes.

Smells of polish and fabric freshener, suddenly sickly and cloying.

The urge to run overcame me.

I dropped the phone in disbelief flicking my hand as if to dislodge the instrument of pain from my hand and ran out of my parent's house. As I ran, from the corner of my eye, I saw my mother emerge from the kitchen into the hall, wiping floury hands on an apron, her mouth moving, but I couldn't hear what she was saying. I don't remember crossing the road or running across grass on the Common, just the moment my feet started to slip and slide on the large pebbles of the beach. I doubled up in pain, as if I had been punched. I heard a feral, guttural, groan of despair that roiled up from my guts and became the high-pitched keening of the gulls. I could not cry. Tears came later.

All that day, I walked the miles between the pier and the old gun battery along the water's edge. The sea rolled in, boiling, swirling, throwing helpless pebbles onto the beach, cruelly sucking them back to be tumbled and beaten again. My mother came to find me, bustling with bracing platitudes, to scoop me up, feed me and tidy the issue away. I wanted her to leave me alone, could she not see? I would shatter like dropped glass if I stopped. Later my Father came silently to walk alongside me, offering no comfort but simply to help bear my burden.

The journey back to Sydney for the funeral was the worst I have ever made. A twenty-four-hour marathon with time inside my own head. In turn I; hated the stupid visa system that made me leave the country to change from a student to a working visa. It was their fault he died. Blamed myself, it was my fault, if I'd have been there maybe he wouldn't have gone up in the plane at all. Felt guilty, maybe I should have been in the plane with him, would that have been better. Raged, that his precious last moments were not spend with me. And on and on, thoughts swirling in my head, preventing anything but the odd dream filled snatches of sleep. Tired and miserable, my hair lank from sleepless nights and grief, skin pale as a winter sky and devoid of make-up, I walked into the Arrivals Hall at Kingston Smith. Annie and Max were there to meet me, for a moment they seemed like people from another life, familiar yet estranged. They seemed slightly awkward in their togetherness, as though it was offensive in the circumstances. But then I saw the dark rings around Max's eyes, his stooped shoulders and Annie's pinched face - she took a faltering step then rushed forward and threw her arms around me. "Ellie, oh Ellie."

Max hung back, but I freed an arm, extending it open and he stepped over encircling us both. We clung to each other, a small island of grief amidst the joyful reunions and the driver pick-ups, sharing our pain and forging the first moments of our new friendship without Brett.

The scene flashing past the car window as we drove across town was normal. The sun shone, glinting on the water as we crossed the bridges and everywhere Jacaranda trees blossomed. People queued for buses or walked, some busy in work suits, others casual in flip flops and shorts. It seemed surreal that so many lives were untouched by the tragedy of Brett's death. I was an extra in their life script, a pale face glimpsed in a passing car, background to the drama of their important interview day or whatever parallel, elaborate epic they were the star of. There were thousands of other lives going on that I would never know about and people who would not mourn Brett's passing. What did I expect? I didn't know, but I hadn't expected the city I loved to look normal.

Outside the flat, I made a brave show of getting out of the car, fussing with my bag and walking down the plant-lined path and through the front door of the block. But then couldn't continue inside.

"Just a minute." I dropped my bag and fled from the front door of the flats heading for an escape in the garden. Taking in gasps of fresh air, another great wave of misery washed over me.

I walked numbly to the end of the garden and sat on the grass with my legs hanging over the end wall, where Sydney Harbour's blue water lapped. I stared blindly across the water. With a snap of fate's fingers, Brett was gone. His strength and vitality erased. His love for life and charm snuffed out. Our future together, washed away as surely as writing in the sand when the tide rolls in.

Sometime later, I heard a soft voice I didn't recognise, "Ellie, can I join you?"

I looked round to see a small, slim lady with a weathered face and unruly grey hair. We had never met, she lived in India, working for an aid organisation, but I had seen many portraits of her: smiling, laughing, serious, eyes full of love, Brett's camera capturing her intelligent, loving spirit. It was Elsa, his mother. I nodded, "Of course, I uhmm..." my voice trailed off. I didn't know what to say.

"Shhh," she bent down to tuck a stray wisp of hair behind my ear, "we both loved him, he loved us - it's enough."

Elsa was generous to me in those few days. She left me to sleep in Brett's room: the one that had become our room. I rolled myself in the sheets that still smelt of him. She selflessly allowed me to pack my favourite photos, his hoodie and peaked sunhat, some of our well-thumbed books and poems and of course the poster of Humphrey Bogart. Her strength, as she grieved, came from her knowledge that she would survive, that she had a cause and a reason to live. She was her own woman as well as his mother. She had already lost him in small ways many times before, in the way that all mothers do as they let their children go towards independence, although I would learn those things with time and life experience, I felt I had lost my entire world and she knew that.

As I arrived at the church for the funeral, I was aware of a blur of faces all looking; looking away, looking down, looking at. Faces, speaking, words.

"Such a shock."

"So sorry."

"Awful."

"If there's anything..."

"Will she stay on?"

Once I reached the calm, sanctuary inside the Chapel, its atmosphere enveloped me and bore my sorrow as it had born the sorrows of many before, absorbing it into wood, stone and light refracted through stained glass. The blur of faces outside was soothed into recognizable groups of friends, colleagues and family, many of whom spoke from the congregation. They shared memories, a funny story, or a poem, simple and spontaneous.

"He was an awesome Photographer. His pictures jumped off the page. He got it all: The image, the emotion, the mood. God bless you Buddy, we're gonna' miss you."

"He loved life, his patients loved him, he made them feel good about themselves, he inspired us. None of us at the clinic can believe he's gone."

Max stood up, his voice vibrant with emotion, "He was my best mate from before school. He knew all my secrets. He had my back and he'd give me a kick up the backside when I needed it. Wherever you are, I love you, you bloody idiot. Why did you go and get yourself killed?" He tried to carry on, but his voice faltered. Annie stretched out her hand and he crumpled into the seat beside her, his frame convulsed by sobs.

In my head, I had words and pictures too, of how we laughed and laughed, walked and talked, loved and studied. How we quarrelled, dark shadows passing across his brown eyes if I was flippant over something he cared about. How much I loved him. But it all remained in my head.

Afterwards, I could not watch him buried. For me, Brett continued as a life force, he was outside, in the air, the sun, the sea, not buried, never buried. I excused myself to Elsa, took a cab into town and walked out to Mrs McQuarry's chair. From there I watched the changing light on the harbour instead.

2. Survival

Still stunned by grief and loss, I returned to England despite Max and Annie's pleas that I stay on and give things a chance in Australia without Brett. I hadn't really cared where I was, when I came back, except I knew I could not be in Sydney. That beautiful but cruel place had robbed me of Brett. I hated the vicious natural beauty that had so fascinated him and ultimately lured him to his death.

After the funeral, I returned to my parent's house on the South coast temporarily. Initially, it was a relief to hand over the day to day concerns of living back to my Mother and to spend days lying in bed staring at the ceiling. My childhood bedroom, still papered with pictures of horses, was my refuge, I emerged only to pick fretfully at food that I simply could not swallow. I refused all offers of 'a nice film', or 'a trip to the shops' to cheer me up. As well as my bedroom, only the deserted beach with its shuttered, deserted huts and gunmetal grey sea, thrashing endlessly at the pebble beach, felt like a place which knew me. After a particularly difficult day, with another of my Mother's pep talks, my wide-eyed stare at her lack of understanding and my Father's crossly muttered "Leave the girl alone Susan, she needs time," I suddenly knew I needed to get away, to get back to work for some normality. I couldn't sustain the awful pain and I had too much time to think. I answered an advert in the Physiotherapy Journal:

"Physiotherapy practice looking for experienced Physiotherapist for maternity cover. Manual Therapy and Acupuncture skills an advantage."

The job was based in Essex, somewhere I'd never been and where no one knew about Brett's death. My grief and everyone's sympathy had become totally disabling. I could've got lost forever in the well-intentioned kindness.

Martin, my new boss was a task master. Due to start at eight on the first morning, he had asked me to arrive at seven thirty, just to settle in.

"Hi Ellie, glad to see you, you've got a busy day today, so you'll need to keep to time. Here's your list."

I stared in some consternation at the page he showed me in the diary, which had a seemingly impossible number of patients entered on it.

"You can work between two rooms. Whilst you are treating in one room, the receptionist will show the next patient into the other and they can change into a gown ready for treatment. That way, you don't waste time whilst they're changing. You have fifteen minutes to treat them, half an hour for a new patient."

Phew! barely time to ask, *'Feeling the same, better or worse after last treatment?'* and treat each patient again. There were some treatments I use regularly, that just wouldn't be possible in the time allocated. But Martin was still talking...

"At the end of treatment, they can change and go out to reception to be re-booked, whilst you swap rooms and get on with the next one. You'll get the idea. Don't run late."

I'd have to be absolutely focused to work so intensively and how would I manage with the patients who needed to be listened to and have time to talk I wondered?

Looking again at the diary page for that day, I said, "I seem to be full from eight this morning until eight this evening with only an hour for lunch."

"No, half an hour for lunch, half an hour for note writing and phone calls. You'll get odd extra spaces, with cancellations on some days."

Slightly doubtful about my ability to manage such a ferocious timetable, but not wanting to seem difficult on my first morning, I said "I'll give it a go, I am used to working with half hour appointments, so until I'm up to speed, I think I may need a quarter of an hour break mid-morning and afternoon to catch up, as well as my lunch break."

He grudgingly agreed, but added, "As long as no one gets turned away."

I started to say "No of course..." But he was off again.

"I've left all the notes up to date in the files, I doubt you'll want to change much in my treatment plans, so you won't need to reassess anyone that I've already seen."

Glancing at the scanty notes he'd made in the patient files, in his cramped, spiky handwriting, I could see that he mainly gave advice and exercise sheets, with an occasional ultrasound treatment or a joint manipulation. Very basic stuff for someone with such impressive qualifications. He clearly wasn't much interested in the people who attended, because his system allowed them so little time. I found it hard to understand. Oh well, at least I'd be busy, which might blot out some of the shell-shocked disbelief and grief that accompanied me everywhere these days and hung over my head like a thick black cloud.

Be careful what you wish for; my new job consisted of twelve-hour days, short appointments and no sympathy at all. The only saving grace was that the relentless pace, and physical exhaustion helped me survive the worst of the early bereavement. I was clearly not my normal self at that time, because it took a year, for me to act on the almost immediate suspicion that working Martin's way wasn't right for me. I'm still not sure why I put myself through it. Perhaps in some perverse way, I was punishing myself for being alive when Brett was dead. Having time for people, talking, trying to understand all aspects of their problem and helping them to feel well, was how I worked, what I believed in. Whatever possessed me to accept his awful de-humanising, conveyor belt work ethic for so long, I can't think. Bereavement clearly distorted my normal functioning and stripped away my confidence, it isn't considered an illness, but it felt like one to me.

In November, Martin called me into the office. I wondered what I had done now; eaten two biscuits at coffee time instead of the designated one? Used too much ultrasound gel? Some other heinous crime... But no, charming as ever when he wanted something, he smiled, "Ellie, Jana would like to go to South Africa for Christmas, to show the baby to her family, before she starts work again. Do you think you could cover the practice alone for a month, to let us get away? It's usually quieter in the New Year."

I was happy to let them get away, Jana had seemed low since the baby was born. "Yes, I can cover, the only thing is, the cottage I'm buying should be ready to complete around then and I'm not sure of my moving date."

The day Martin and Jana left, he popped in to the clinic and said "About your move..." I expected him to say "Don't worry if you have to take a couple of days off," but instead he said, "Make sure you don't take any time off."

I had picked up over the year, that he was a self-centred person and very money orientated, but his remark took my breath away, talk about 'looking a gift horse in the mouth'. When I thought back to the caring relationship I had had with Brett and how much he loved people, Martin's hard boiled, critical attitude shocked me. But it wasn't just that, I had overheard him being patronising and dismissive to some of his female patients and he adopted a very dictatorial and bullying attitude to our admin. colleagues too. His slight disdain for perceived weakness in anyone, gave me chills. Martin and I were not a great fit at any level but his misogyny was unsettling. I wasn't sure what it could lead him to do if crossed. Jana was such a kind and gentle soul, which is perhaps how she managed to cope with being married to him, because any normal person would have run screaming in the other direction.

I doubted very much that he was faithful to her. Several veiled remarks made by my patients had already alluded to the fact he was a player. It's hard to keep secrets in a small town and Jana was the youngest daughter of this particular town's monied "Royalty", so people seemed to look at them and their doings with particular interest, almost a living soap opera. I couldn't think why she had, but she had married him. I suddenly felt lucky, what on earth was I doing here? I could leave. The thought made me feel lighter, why on earth hadn't I thought about leaving before, there were plenty of other jobs in this area, I didn't envy Jana one bit.

As I saw Martin clearly for the first time, I realised with a pang, like a knife in my stomach, that I had found a total gem of a person in Brett; funny, loving, confident, interesting. I doubted I'd find two like that in a lifetime, and I wasn't settling for less. I'd rather be alone to the end of my days, which seemed increasingly likely.

When my moving date fell within the time Martin and Jana were away, and I felt obligated not to close the clinic at all, Dad and Mum arrived without saying any of the things they were thinking. How Dad muzzled Mum, I'll never know. They moved my things from my rented flat, into the cottage, whilst I worked and kept the practice running without a break.

It was my Dad that inadvertently put the idea of setting up my own clinic into my head.

"This is a lovely little town, with all the new building, it looks a bit raw, but there seems to be a good community growing here. Lots of young couples about with children, I think it will mature into a very nice place. Is there a Physio practice here? That chap you're working with at the moment doesn't seem very nice if you don't mind my saying."

"No there isn't and you're right, he's the pits." After doing my course in Australia, I didn't really want to go back into hospital, I liked having a bit more freedom in the clinics I worked in out there. "Martin's clinic is too impersonal for me."

"Oh well sweetheart, you'll have to look around, I'm sure you'll find something."

Mum chipped in with, "Sometimes you just have to get on with things, you've got a nice little cottage now, so working with Martin hasn't been all bad, you can't have your cake and eat it you know. Although, a steady hospital job might be better for later on, if you have children..." She tailed off as I gave her a ferocious look, she was so tactless sometimes.

The final straw that pushed me to take the plunge, were the horrible things Martin said the day he asked me to stay on for longer in the clinic because Jana wasn't ready to come back to work.

"You've done fairly well for yourself here, made the most of a fantastic opportunity. As you know, I can help you earn lots of money and at least you seem to be able to put in a decent day's work without moaning, unlike my wife."

Jana had already told me, rather tearfully, over a cup of coffee, that she didn't feel ready to return to work and that Martin may ask me to stay on. Who could blame her? The baby had yet to sleep through one night, she must have been exhausted.

"She's got a good dose of lazy-itis if you ask me, Jana isn't doing anything, just mooning over the baby. She isn't back to running or the gym and she's turning into a hippopotamus. She is starting to remind me of some of my patients."

I ignored the last patronizing comment with difficulty and said, "Surely, you don't think she is being lazy? She's a lovely, intelligent girl dealing with an unsettled baby and chronic sleep deprivation. Give her time..."

"Plenty of women around the world give birth in the morning and are back at work in the fields by the afternoon. But not her, she just mopes about, I don't know what she does all day, the house isn't always tidy even! She'll have no brain left at all if she stays at home."

Always a full of himself and apt to believe his own PR, I was nonetheless shocked, it clearly hadn't occurred to him she was struggling to cope. As I looked into his eyes which showed not an ounce of compassion for Jana, I couldn't help but compare. I remembered Brett tears running down his cheeks as he showed me some photographs,

"Oh, Ellie look, how beautiful they are and so young, still children themselves."

It was a series of pictures he had taken of nomadic Arabic girls. During their largely unassisted births, many of them sustained pelvic floor tears, which left them incontinent. As a result, they were often abandoned.

"These women are beautiful Ellie, their bodies are beautiful, they have given birth, they are not unclean."

His photographs had been part of an awareness drive, to fund a team of Physio's to go out and teach basic pelvic floor rehabilitation to the local staff at a refuge.

It seemed obvious to me that Jana may also have post-natal depression and wondered why the thought hadn't occurred to Martin.

"She needs to get over it, get a Nanny and get back to work."

"Would you like me to have a chat? I think she may need a bit more support, but as she is used to being a good coper, she hasn't realised"

"No! Don't you go sympathising and encouraging her to be all weepy and pathetic. She's much better if I ignore it. That's what I've told her friends as well, too much talking about how she feels isn't good for her. She's just got to man up! I'm the one you should be having a sympathetic chat to, she's left me high and dry with a business to run, I was banking on her being back at work by now, time is money."

I made a mental note that I'd have that chat with her, despite his moronic attitude, poor girl.

I began to understand why he was happy to work short appointments, no space for people to talk about their worries or problems... Every patient was just a unit sale to him, not a real person. I tried one last time to get through, "We're all different and lots of women have plans to return to work quickly, but feel differently when the baby arrives. Jana hasn't been off for six months yet, give her a chance."

"Well, I can't carry dead wood forever, she'll have to buck up soon."

I was speechless with horror, but rapidly discovered as well as being insensitive, Martin could get very angry. When I politely turned his offer down to stay longer, maybe permanently, at the practice, any charm he had expended on me, rapidly disappeared. He realised he wasn't going to get his own way and rounded on me.

"You'll regret this, letting me down. You won't get a great offer like this every day."

I found myself blurting out, "I would like to work nearer to my new home. There isn't a Physiotherapist there yet and I would like to set something up." There, the half idea that had been in my head was out. Working as I wanted to, without someone else dictating to me how many times I could see someone or how long an appointment should last, appealed to me.

"If you think you can just walk away and steal my patients to set up on your own, you're mistaken because I'll sue."

"Martin, I have no intention of stealing any patients, it is at least fifteen miles away and in a different health authority catchment, so completely different Doctor referrals and too far for your patients to want to travel. I shall be building up my own clientele gradually. My own temper started to flare, who did he think he was attacking my professionalism?

"What would you sue me for? I am not in breach of my contract with you, I shall be working well outside the exclusion zone you put in it."

“Well don’t come running to me when you’re bankrupt, it takes more than Physio training and a pretty face to run a successful business.” Red faced, with a vein pulsing in his forehead he almost spat “Get your things and go, I don’t want you accessing my client files before you leave.”

Face burning with the sting of his words and the injustice, I collected my things and left, without even the chance to say good bye to the receptionists, who had all been so kind to me.

The anger didn’t last long, what on earth had I done? How was I going to pay the mortgage? I worried about my patients too, at least during my time at Martin’s clinic, I had been able to treat them kindly, not like bugs under a microscope, despite the time constraints. One lovely lady, Louise, that I had seen for the first time that morning, was so stressed. She was a case in point, she needed someone to talk to and coach her about pacing her life a bit better, just as much as she needed physiotherapy for her pain. If what I’d heard today was anything to go by, she’d be told to “Man up!” by Martin. Hopefully, she’d spit in his eye and find somewhere more caring to have her treatment. Delivering an efficient technical treatment wasn’t the whole story. “Time is money,” unbelievable! I never thought I would hear a Physio say those words.

Mum predictably had a melt-down prophesying all manner of doom and disaster. She didn’t need to, inwardly, I was panicking enough myself.

“Get yourself an agency job to tide you over and have a proper think about this project Ellie. Why don’t you talk to your Uncle James?” Dad was referring to my Godfather, James, honorary Uncle and successful businessman. He gave me a hug, “Don’t worry about your Mother, you know she frets, we both believe in you. Do what’s right for you love.”

I found a place to begin working for myself in my new ‘home’ town. It was rather cramped and on the first floor with no lift, which wasn’t ideal for some of my patients, but it was a start and affordable. Two rented rooms with a cupboard sized tearoom and a tiny toilet, on top of the shoe shop in the town square. I worked crazy hours on a shoestring budget, teaching and doing agency work as well, to make ends meet, for three years whilst I got established. If I’m honest, during those three years, I was still running from my shock and despair at losing Brett too.

Then, six months ago, a hammer blow fell in the form of a curt letter. The shoe shop was closing, the building had been sold to Developers and I would no longer be able to rent my rooms. What? All my hard work and now no premises. My safe place, my bolt hole, gone. Seeing me like a headless chicken, my Godfather James, had once again offered to look at my figures for the last three years. He helped me draft a new business plan and suggested I talk to the banks about a possible business loan, which would allow me to invest in the business and continue in my own premises. It all made sense.

In the ensuing six months, there were tough negotiations for the loan to buy and equip the new premises. Those meetings with Bank Managers still gave me night terrors. Like Martin, they didn't care about the people, only about the money. I wasn’t stupid, I did understand that to remain open, the Clinic books had to balance and I had to be able to live, but they seemed to have no concept of the therapeutic needs of the venture. Surely, I could achieve both?

Generous support in the form of a personal loan from my Godfather, meant I could keep any bank loan, with its crippling interest, to a reasonable size. The long, difficult search for a suitable building, one which the council planning department would approve for medical usage, seemed to take forever. There were times when I wondered if I was doing the right thing and if I would ever get there. I felt exhausted and disheartened. In my lowest moments, I heard Brett's voice in my head, "Go for your dream Ells." I had decided to call the new clinic, if it ever materialised, 'Touch.' Statement of rebellion against Martin's hands-off approach and because I believed in the therapeutic properties of touch at the heart of my treatments, *we* had; Brett and I.

Rose, my amazing admin. colleague, loyal supporter from day one at the shoe shop, reception genius and all-round treasure; along with Pen, my best friend, had kept me sane through the long process. Finally, we were about to move into our own dedicated clinic space and Rose would have a proper office and reception, I think she was as excited as I was, but she would never have let on. With her neat brown hair perfectly in place, conservative clothes and economical manner, Rose remained dignified at all times, but she didn't fool me.

My hard work during those years above the shoe shop had not been wasted. From being a total unknown in the area, I seemed to be gaining a good reputation. We had a steady trickle of Doctor and Consultant referrals and thankfully, lots of word of mouth recommendations. If things continued to go well, I hoped to have enough work for a colleague to join me one day in the future and now I would have space for that to happen. I shivered, setting up alone had been a white-knuckle, roller coaster ride, there had been more than a few times when I thought I might end up bankrupt, just as Martin said I would. With all the extra costs in the new premises, it was still a distinct possibility. The nasty little voice of doubt that plagued me in the early hours of the morning, when I lay awake worrying, once again whispered spitefully "You must be mad." I ignored it, as I had more or less managed to do over the last three years, and kept doggedly working hard, sticking to Brett's maxim that '*you make your own luck*.' I saw myself as a young sapling, tentatively pushing its way upwards, growing stronger, branching out, vulnerable still, but managing so far to survive.

I wanted to write to Martin to tell him how wrong he'd been about me. Pretty face indeed, bloody cheek! Hard work and a leap of faith had got me this far, now the buck stopped with me to continue to make Touch successful. I set my shoulders square, I wasn't giving up any time soon. Somehow, the success of the practice had come to represent my own recovery, I wasn't sure how I'd manage, if it failed.

3. Moving.

Over the course of the day we, myself, Rose and Jem, her long-suffering husband, dismantled and packed everything from the rooms above the shoe shop. Rain fell in torrents all day, cascading over the gutters and splashing up inches off the pavers in the town square. We felt the Gods were laughing. Moving everything the next day in the sodden weather was going to be a challenge. However, with no choice, we continued to open cupboards and drawers, wrapping and stacking everything neatly in boxes and labelling it; "kitchen", "office", "treatment room" as appropriate. How much stuff can you fit into one small place? I wondered, as I sealed up yet another box and wrote its label. The move had to be complete over the weekend, I simply couldn't afford to miss another working day. My estimate of what it would cost to move had already proved to be optimistic.

Finally, the last box containing the diary, patient notes for Monday, the desk top stuff and pens was labelled "first box to unpack" and we were ready to move out.

On Saturday morning, I had my first surprise of the day, some of the rugby lads from the local club, appeared one by one to help lift the incredibly heavy, awkward hydraulic couch, the furniture and boxes and manhandle them down the stairs. I looked at Rose and she shrugged "Jem asked them to come, you do lots for them and they're happy to help out."

Several of the lads looked like green-hued ghosts and were sporting massive hangovers, but bless them they had turned out regardless. Rose had provided trays of croissants and vats of coffee, more trays of sandwiches for later and lots of snacks. She believed in feeding growing lads. Under her watchful eye, one team of helpers loaded my precious physio equipment into the small van I'd borrowed from a patient and then packed boxes around the couch swathed in Jem's dust sheets. The rest of us moved off to the new premises and unloaded at the other end, stowing boxes as best we could into their designated place. The van ploughed a furrow for most of the morning between the old premises and the new. We lugged and lifted, stacked and stored like professionals.

I couldn't help noticing as we were stacking boxes into the new premises, that Gary, one of the Forwards kept rubbing his neck and stretching after each lift. "What have you done there?" I asked.

"Oh, it's nothing Ellie, got a crunching tackle a couple of weeks ago, but I'm alright. Seem to be able to play through it but it's painful for a couple of days after."

When I was at the club, I did my best to teach the players how to stretch, that balance and agility exercises had value and that doing more than just play rugby in pre-season training sessions would benefit their performance. Although I convinced a few of them to treat injuries seriously and not play on damaged tissues, it was swimming upstream against the current.

"Let me see."

As I moved behind him, I was aware of his compact and powerful frame, but also how tight and short some of his muscles were. His arms stuck out like wings and his neck had virtually disappeared into his shoulders because of the imbalance. The extra weight he was carrying didn't help either. Feeling along the top of both shoulders, I picked up a really knotted lump on the left.

"Wow! The muscle running from your neck down to your shoulder is very tight, so is this one," I said, pressing another knot in the belly of Supraspinatus, one of the rotators of the shoulder.

"Ouch, steady on Ellie," he winced as I pressed.

"I just want to check if that muscle on your shoulder could be torn."

"OK, no probs." A quick resisted muscle test, which showed up weakness, made me think he had possibly damaged the rotator cuff of the shoulder and maybe his neck too.

"I've only had a quick look, but you've got a bit of an injury here, I think you ought to let me assess this properly."

"Oh, really? I reckon a couple of games will kill or cure it. I'll knock off the training sessions."

"Not a great idea Gary, probably safer to do the training and some rehab exercises for your shoulder, but knock off the matches for a couple of weeks."

He looked at me as if I had two heads "I can't let the team down!"

"You might put yourself out for the whole season if you don't look after it. Look, if I can find the right box in all this muddle, let me at least tape it up for you and then you could try to get in for a proper treatment session as soon as you can. Any allergies to sticky tape like plasters?"

He shook his head, "No, think I'm fine."

As I rummaged in one of the boxes and balanced a container of powder on the side, it toppled, I tried to catch it and a great puff exploded out across the floor. "What a mess!" I dusted the powder off my hands onto my jeans. He headed off to get a broom, but I called him back, "Don't worry about it, I'll clear up later." I managed to find a roll of sports tape in one of the boxes, but no razor, "This will pull a bit when it comes off because I can't shave the hair off your shoulder, you're not too hairy though, is that OK?"

"Yeah, go for it, my girlfriend will love ripping that off. I can see her paying off a few scores already."

I laughed, "Give it a soak in the bath first, that'll help. It should stay on for at least two or three days. Take it off earlier if it starts to make your skin itch or it isn't making the shoulder more comfortable though."

Once the tape was in place, I retested the muscle, it tested stronger so maybe it wasn't torn after all just weak because of the pain. He said it felt better, "Thanks Ellie, that's magic."

"My good deed for the day, thank you for all your help as well."

When the old rooms were clear, we locked up at the new place and all joined forces back above the Shoe Shop to attack it with hoovers, dusters, mops and buckets, a good spring clean. Finally, dirty, tired, but satisfied by a good job done, we went back to Touch's new home for a last coffee and because the lads were hungry again!

The new home of the clinic was a two bedroomed, detached bungalow in the old part of town, close to the station. As we squeezed into the small kitchen, the rugby guys overfilled it, with someone leaning against every available surface. Rugby players come in all different shapes and sizes and we had a fair representation of that draped around the kitchen. They seemed so carefree, eating and chatting, I on the other hand, under my calm exterior, felt sick with fear that I'd overextended myself and my dream would not work out. My nerves jangled like the cans behind a honeymoon car. "Get a grip," I thought crossly.

As the lads polished off the last of the food, they double-checked there was nothing else to lift and then left, heading for a good night out.

"Thanks guys, you've been great today. I really appreciate it. We would have struggled without you."

"No worries Ellie, these guys need to lose a bit of weight, 'specially Gazza." one joked.

"Yeah right mate, you know it's all muscle," he replied, lifting his shirt to reveal a copious spare tyre and a hairy belly.

"That's gross! Cover it up! Hey Ellie, we're going for a Chinese then out to Southend clubbing tonight. Why don't you come with us, be fun, some of the girls are coming too, last night was lad's only night."

It would've been nice to join them, it was a while since I'd been out in a big crowd - well not since Sydney really. But, I declined, despite their kind offer. I needed to collect my dogs from the farm where they had been looked after by my friend Pen and collapse in a tired heap on the sofa with a mug of cocoa.

"See," one of them said "you've put her off with your fat belly," prodding the culprit.

I could hear them laughing and bantering as they strolled off in the direction of the Rugby Club and I realised that they had unwittingly made me feel lonely.

I shooed Rose and Jem away soon after the lads. They offered to start unpacking, but having looked dubiously at all the boxes, I realised that I just wanted to be on my own for a while. I'd had enough for today. All this was a far cry from the life I'd imagined for myself in Sydney with Brett and sometimes I felt as if I was still acting out a life, not properly living it. Trying to be positive, I told myself I was my own boss, caring for people in my own style and I'd needed permanent premises that suited the way I worked for some time. Dulling the brightness of my achievements, was survivor guilt. I was, despite everything, beginning to move on and make plans that Brett and I had never considered together. He would never have the chance to fulfil any of his dreams and, all my caring for other people could never bring him back. I missed him, his zest for life and support. I wanted him to still be here, to share all these good things with me. The thought made me angry, "Why? Why did he go up in that stupid plane? And, why that particular day?"

Keeping my thoughts to myself, I said to Rose, "I think we've done enough, let's call it a day and unpack tomorrow."

For the first time, I was alone in my new practice and looked about. Surely if I worked hard enough and made this place amazing, I could exorcise my ghosts and move on? Guilt washed over me for thinking it, "Never, I won't ever forget him." I said out loud.

I padded from room to room, the bedrooms, now converted to treatment rooms, glowed softly with newly painted, creamy-white walls. Beautiful oak floorboards, retrieved for me from a building being demolished by a patient, looked rich with mature colour and muffled my footsteps. Although a bit expensive, they had been too beautiful to let go. Neutral blinds at the windows created a subtle light and my favourite landscape photos from Brett's collections would soon be on the walls, *he will be here with me,* I thought defiantly. I caught sight of myself in the mirrored wall, neither tall, nor fashionably waif like, I am more medium height with hour-glass curves. In the soft light my skin glowed resolutely pale and without mascara I look like an albino rabbit. As a child, my grandmother explained my hazel eyes to me, "God ran out of paint, so he used a bit from all the pots for you."

Wavy, red hair and freckles scattered across my nose like autumn leaves gave me an outdoorsy look. All things considered, I liked my body, it wasn't perfect, whose is? But I don't want to swap with anyone. I didn't think this lightly. As a Physio I saw more bodies than most people. Bodies disclose secrets about the life they've led and prophesy what may happen in the future... For better, for worse, this body was mine and had my life so far etched into every curve. At thirty, I had begun to feel comfortable with it.

There was a theme to the clinic décor, inspired from Chinese Five Elements theory. Brett's landscape photos would represent the Earth element and give a grounded feel to the rooms. I imagined myself giving acupuncture treatments in this calm space, tealights warming aromatherapy burners. Moxa, the herb burnt over acupuncture needles to provide gentle heat when treating long-standing or arthritic conditions, would provide the uplifting energy that the Fire element brings. The theory is that if you act it, you become it and I could do with some calm and some uplifting for myself. I was far from sure that I could sustain the loan repayments and although James had airily said I could borrow his money for as long as I needed to, I wondered how he would feel if I went bankrupt and lost the lot.

New ornaments, small reproductions of beautiful dance sculptures by Rodin, brought the Metal element, balancing grief and loss. I held one for a moment feeling its smooth curves, perhaps they would bring balance for me too. I was still spending far too much time alone crying, my relationship with Brett had been so fabulous and had burned bright, but like a sparkler on bonfire night it had been short lived. Acceptance of his death didn't bring much comfort though and I missed him, I missed him terribly, what can I say? If I were my patient, I'd think I was in a state of unresolved grief. But did I really want it resolved? If that meant letting Brett go, I wasn't sure I did and the thought of being close to anyone else... I couldn't imagine it. Who? Someone like Martin? I'd rather die, slime-ball!

Ready to leave, I checked the windows to see they were all locked - on warm days, when they were open, a breeze would flow through the building. Although not one of the main five elements, Wind, in Chinese medicine, is nevertheless an important influence on people, essential to bringing change and movement. My footsteps barely sounded on my beautiful wood floor, its calming effect, soothed me as I moved from room to room and I carefully pushed my anger back into its' box, from which it only ever escaped when I was by myself.

Finishing my tour, I heard the water bubbling in a small feature in reception and gave a wry smile as I bent to switch it off. The water element was to balance fear, shock and overwork. That little water feature needed to punch above its weight, overwork was my survival mechanism. I didn't have all these dark thoughts when I was working.

The idea that we feel well and healthy when the flow and balance of our life is right, appeals to me. The early Chinese practitioners didn't have the scientific tests and scanning instruments we have at our disposal today, to help with diagnosis. Their treatments and care principles came from close observation of many people, over many years. Any medical diagnosis is about recognition of patterns, and the Chinese patterns offer treatment pathways in addition to our Western Medicine ones. It's great to have both. If I was ever to re-find my own balance surely it would be here? Honestly, I wasn't convinced that I would ever have another lover apart from my work. Could I leave myself open to the pain again for one thing?

'Had I really borrowed twenty thousand pounds to have my own premises? The thought came unbidden into my mind and my mouth felt dry all of a sudden, it was a lot of money.'

Only this morning, one of the heavier rugby lads had perched on a windowsill and it had cracked. The wood seemed rotten, so everyone felt there must be a leak somewhere. I ran my hands through my hair and massaged my tight temples for a moment, breathing deeply to push that fear down, more money to get it repaired. I decided not to think about it today and to head off before I talked myself into a blue funk. I switched off all the lights, checked the windows and gathered up my bag. 'Touch Physiotherapy Clinic'; I stepped out and looked up at the sign carrying my new logo above the door. I'd chosen a graceful willow tree, its branches brushing a symbolic river whose curves resembled a spine. Locking the door, I turned away, headed for the car and onward to the farm where my best friend Pen lived with her husband Angus, in one of the stockman's houses.

It was to say the least, a bit rickety and freezing. The only warm place was the kitchen, which was cluttered and homely and housed amongst other things two Pointers called Belle and Daisy and two sleek grey cats. Pen and I had met through our dogs and had been firm friends ever since. Pen and Angus met working in London, but Angus's Dad, who owned the farm, had a heart attack, so Angus left his city job to work with him. He was gradually taking over the running of the farm with Pen helping him, his Father had almost retired.

I felt a pang of envy, as I saw two sets of wellies by the door, the his and hers undies drying over the airer in the boot-room and the clutter of coats, some large, some small, which jostled on coat hooks; casual, cruel reminders of what might have been for me too.

Jeeves and Bird, were ecstatic to see me. They exploded out of Pen's kitchen in a tumble of glossy black coats, with swishing, chestnut feathers, as if they'd been abandoned forever in conditions of extreme hardship, not as I strongly suspected, having been holed up on Pen's sofa after a long walk, with an odd tasty snack thrown in along the way.

"Hi Pen," I called over the excited rumpus.

"Hi there, come in, if you can untangle yourself. Cuppa? Glass of wine?"

"I could murder a cup of tea thanks, but I won't stay long. I'm completely shattered, so if I linger, I may end up asleep on your sofa. I'm filthy too, can't believe how much newspaper print and dust I've got on me."

"Yep, you're looking pretty grimy, I was too polite to mention it. In fact, you have a very fetching streak of something all down one cheek, not to mention white hand-prints on your bum – whose are they?"

I quickly squinted in the mirror by the door then turned my rear to check, sure enough, I was sporting a grey smudge from under my right eye to my temple, obviously from running my hands, black from newspaper ink, up through my hair and there were two white handprints.

"Now I look closer, it looks like the hand-prints are yours," Pen said, shaking her head in mock disappointment. "No grappling in the store cupboard with one of the rugby lads then?"

"Yeah right Pen, especially looking so glam!"

"You'd look great if you fell in a swamp, you just don't realise it and its time you found yourself a man again," she chided, as she handed me a cup of my favourite green tea scented with cardamom pods. I could see her warming to a favourite topic as she patted the slightly saggy sofa that sat on one side of the kitchen, inviting me to sit.

"It's OK, I'll prop up the Aga for a moment, the warmth feels nice, it'll ease up my muscles. Crikey we worked hard today."

"Don't change the subject," she wagged her finger, "you've got to try again sometime, and if the number of toads I kissed before I found Angus is anything to go by, you need to get going."

I was too tired to be nagged, "I can't Pen, not just now. I feel, oh I don't know, disloyal to Brett, not ready, whatever. I don't think there will ever be another Brett. Anyway, I'm much too busy right now."

"Hun, love like you've never been hurt and all that...It's been four years."

It was alright for her to say that, she'd found her *Mr Right*. Angus was her friend, lover and husband all rolled into one. Four years ago, I thought I'd found my soul-mate too and I *had* been hurt. I wasn't sure I could go through that again. Sometimes I felt like Brett had abandoned me. Why had he died? He was thirty, talented and my lover. Idiot! And, where did that leave me? Standing in the middle of my shattered dreams, that's where. Despite the anger that flared inside me, I knew Pen had a point and what's more Brett would say the same - *C'mon Ells, do it*, *C'mon Ells, got nothing to lose*, or even, his favourite, *C'mon Ells you'll regret the things you don't do, not the things you've done.*

Close to tears, I headed her off the scent with a white lie, "OK, OK! I'll think about finding a new man, but not tonight. I'm too tired for anything but a bath, the telly, and my bed. Thanks again for having the dogs, they'd have been so bored at home. You're sure you don't mind having them again tomorrow?"

"Not a problem, it does mine good to mix with the riff raff sometimes!"

"Cheeky mare! Riff raff indeed! Look at my noble hounds."

We both looked down to where they were disposed elegantly at my feet exuding grace and aristocracy.

"Yes, well you wouldn't have said that earlier if you'd seen the state of Bird. She rolled in fox poo then managed to wipe it on Jeeves and my two. Whatever they look like now, they're a pair of low-lives."

"Sorry Pen, what a nightmare... I'll take them away."

"Look take this and warm it up," she pressed a Tupperware into my hand from the fridge, "it's only cottage pie but I bet you've been eating snacky stuff all day."

I pressed a big kiss on her cheek. She touched a raw nerve every now and then, but it was only because she cared about me. "Thank you, thank you, you're a lifesaver. I'm not even going to politely dissemble, I shall wolf it down and lick the tub."

Whistling up my two dogs, I loaded them into the car, jumped in and, waving through the window, headed on home. Later, soaking in the bath, I thought about what Pen had said. She was right, I thought reluctantly, perhaps I did need to move on with my personal life or at least try to. Despite work, friends and dogs, I was often lonely. Maybe that would change if I had the intimacy which comes with a partner. But I hadn't met anyone since Brett died that even tempted me. It was one thing for Pen to nag me about looking for a new boyfriend, but they didn't grow on trees, and she hadn't come up with anyone, for all her talk. Where did you go to meet a bloke these days? I had no idea.

I realised the bath was getting cold around me and hopped out. Towelling off, I put on PJ's and my sheepskin slippers, now slightly chewed at the front on one side thanks to Bird. I'd bought them in one of the touristy shops close to the Opera House and Brett had teased me mercilessly about being conned. Oh well, that's one thing he was wrong about, I loved them, lived and died in them when I was at home and they didn't owe me a penny. I went down the steep stairs, almost a ladder, from my room to the sitting room, let the dogs out and settled them for the night, before climbing back up to my bedroom in the roof and falling thankfully into bed.

4. New Friends.

Next morning, I woke with a start, feeling that I'd overslept. In fact, when I looked at the clock it was only six thirty. The roof light above the bed showed a square of blue sky, across which a plane glinted in the sun and left a white vapour trail. I yawned, my little cottage was a bit of a dolls house, but enough for me on my own. Squeezed between two larger houses in a terrace of three, it did have a surprising long, narrow garden that gave onto fields. It was also affordable! Very necessary attribute now I'd moved the practice. I felt that familiar flutter of nerves as I thought about the loan from the bank and the one from my Godfather James. I had never borrowed money before.

I swear I hadn't yet moved, but by some telepathy, I could hear sounds of the dogs stirring expectantly downstairs. I smiled as I heard Bird craft a theatrical yawn, which finished with a prolonged whine. There was time for a quick walk before I went back to my unpacking at the clinic, so I threw on some comfortable clothes. As I opened the kitchen door, a riot greeted me, both dogs squirming, wagging, turning in circles to rub against me and making delighted "Woo-Woo" noises.

"Morning guys! Hey handsome boy - hey gorgeous girl!" I ruffled their heads as I made my way to the kettle. "Enough, enough, GUYS"! I struggled to walk through them to fill it at the sink and said "No teeth!" as Birdie tried to mouth the sleeve of my fleece, an old puppy trick that resurfaced in moments of excitement. I glanced at the clock, a quick cup of coffee then time to go. I still had plenty to do at Touch.

"Right." The magic word! Both dogs headed for the gate, feathered tails pluming.

"Just a short one today though, your Auntie Pen will take you for a long walk later."

They seemed happy to settle for that, any walk was a good walk in their book. They accompanied me round the park and took off along the hedge at a gallop, black coats gleaming, feathers streaming behind them and ears bouncing gleefully. Pen's words from last night still echoed around my head, and the night had brought no counsel. I felt at a complete loss as to where I might meet someone. I wondered if any of Angus' Young Farmer friends were single and reluctantly decided that I may have to ask for Pen's help. The walk blew away the cobwebs and after I loaded them back into the car, the dogs and I headed for the farm.

Angus was on the drive at the front of the house as I drew up, chatting to a couple of guys I didn't recognise. "Hi Ellie, meet Dominic and Mark. Mark has bought the barn, you know the one along the road past our boundary. He plans to renovate it and he'll need access through our land for some of the work."

"Hi! Pleased to meet you." As I slid off of the truck's high seat, I extended my hand in greeting and took in their nice 'country' clothes and expensive wellies, the kind I only wear for special occasions. I felt a bit shabby in my unpacking gear.

"Angus tells us you're busy moving and what a great Physio you are... Magic hands he tells us!" Dominic said.

Brett had taught me, in exasperation at my foolish tendency to be self-deprecating, to accept compliments graciously. '*Don't bat compliments away or go all meek and self-conscious, smile and say thank you.*' So, I smiled at Dominic and said "Thank you, Angus is a great PR guy, very affordable too!"

To my credit, I managed to hold eye contact steadily, even though I could feel a flush creeping up my neck. Short and slender but wiry looking at the same time, Dominic had sandy, blonde hair and a Celtic skin. But it wasn't Dominic who was making me blush, despite his compliments. He wasn't really my type, but the other one... I was slightly shocked at the thought: I'd imagined that department of my brain was indefinitely on strike. It seemed not.

In the periphery of my vision, I checked out Mark. He had a mop of curly, dark hair, a loose-limbed look and smooth, tanned skin. Quieter than his friend, he seemed more reserved. But I noticed, as we shook hands, that his charming, shy, smile completely lit his face. If I'd been in the market for a new man... But I wasn't. I wasn't totally immune either, I felt a bit breathless and flustered all of a sudden.

"Nice to meet you," I said to both guys, "good luck with the barn Mark." He was going to be Pen's neighbour, so we'd probably meet again. Still, I thought, as I wasn't really convinced about being in the market for a new man, it didn't matter one way or the other.

I let the dogs into the farmhouse kitchen and put their raw food in the fridge, then with a ruffle around the neck for both, left them to Pen's battered sofa and went around to the back of the farmhouse. Pen was there in denim dungarees and a stripy tee shirt clipping branches off the hedge for the goats to nibble at. She waved as I approached and looked all rosy and full of health. "Hey Ellie, dogs settled?"

"Yup, their food's in the fridge – ox heart, chicken wings and some berries, yum!"

"Mmmm, don't let Angus see that stuff, he'll be frying it up for breakfast!" Then, all breezy and casual she asked "Did you meet the guys? They are going to be our new neighbours. I thought they seemed nice, really friendly."

I couldn't resist, "What the gay couple?"

Pen looked ludicrously disappointed. "Oh, do you think they're gay?"

"Pen, I love you, I can read you like a book and I don't know if they're a couple, I just said hello to them!"

"I don't know what you mean Ellie," she remonstrated, "I was only thinking..." Her voice trailed off.

"I know exactly what you were thinking! And I'm off! Before you have me paired off to one of those poor unsuspecting guys. You should start your own dating agency, Hun."

"Listen, Ellie," she called after me, "I'm doing a roast tonight, eat with us when you're finished, save you bothering about anything as you're busy all day."

"I wouldn't say no, Pen, are you sure that's OK?"

"Yes! No probs, aim for six, but if you're not finished, let me know and I'll keep a plate warm for you."

"Brilliant, I'll see you later. I'll bring wine."

Rounding the corner of the house again, the three men were still deep in conversation, so I just waved as I jumped into the car and headed off for the practice. I was way too busy to think about Mark or Dominic again for the rest of that day, except to wonder if they would be sociable when Mark moved in? I even wondered if Dominic would be around at all, he may just be Mark's Estate Agent or his Architect for all I knew. However, they seemed about my age and hadn't I just been thinking about where people met a new man? Suddenly awash with the horrible sensation I was contemplating cheating on Brett, I swallowed hard and pushed Mark la-de-da and his mate Dom firmly out of my mind. Fate, in the form of Pen was about to bring them back to my notice however.

Unpacking at the practice went smoothly, we had done most of the sorting and clearing at the old place, so although it was back breaking and we all got covered in newspaper ink again, the place was pretty much sorted and ready for work by four o'clock. Jem, was just connecting up the phones, one on the front desk and one in my little study. Rose double checked the word processor was still functioning after the move, and printed the diary for tomorrow morning.

As we finished, I ran out to my car, I had flowers for Rose, and I gave her and Jem a voucher for a meal at the local "posh" restaurant "Clouds," as an extra thank you for giving up their week end. Rose scolded, she was right, I couldn't really afford it, but I could see she was touched, and they were both worth their weight in gold. I was being honest when I said I didn't know where I'd be without them.

I popped home to tidy up before I went to Pen's for dinner. The rain of yesterday gone, today felt clean and fresh and I hummed a little tune to myself, pleased the move had gone as planned. A quick shower, clean jeans and a sweater pulled on, a flick of mascara added and I headed for Pen's and the promise of a roast dinner.

As I pulled up in front of the farm, there was a car I didn't recognise. It was a huge four by four, gleaming, without so much as a speck of mud on it. A sharp contrast to my battered dog car and Pen's aged Landrover. Through the kitchen window, I saw the taller, darker of the two guys I'd seen earlier this morning, Mark. 'Playing at being the country squire, with his posh car - well he isn't fooling anyone, country cars have mud on them!' I thought, 'What's he still doing here anyway?' Then it came to me, and I muttered, "Hmm, Pen up to her tricks!" If Pen was trying to set me up with some awful, get rich quick, city boy who fancied playing at country living, I might just go home. I can't stand those idiots. I had to go in, to say thank you at the very least, I also needed to collect my dogs.

I tapped on the door and pushed it open. Slipping my shoes off, I stepped in, expecting to be flattened by Jeeves and Bird but there was no sign of them. "Hi Pen, Angus."

"Hi, Ellie, just in time, grab a glass of wine, you remember Mark?"

I nodded and put my wine contribution on the table, flashing Pen an exasperated look which she pretended not to see, I cursed my pale skin which flushed so rosily at my hypocrisy, after what I'd just been thinking in the car, "Hi, Mark."

"How did it go today?" Said Pen.

"Yes, it all went well, think I'm ready to start tomorrow."

"Dogs are out in the kennels. They all went in the pond, so they're drying off under the heat lamps. Go out if you want to."

Tempting, this could have been the way out of a terrible evening with city boy, but the smell of roast beef won out and my tummy was rumbling... "Think I'll stay clean till we've eaten!" I laughed. "No Dominic?" I said to Mark.

"No, he works away a lot, he's flying out to the States early tomorrow for two weeks, so he's gone back up to London. He's put some money in the barn as an investment, but it's my project, he's based in London. I'll be here permanently, using it to live and work from."

"How do you guys know one another? Do you work together?" Pen asked from her position at the Aga where various saucepans were bubbling merrily and that fabulous smell of roast beef emanated.

"No, we've been best friends since school." I flashed Pen a teasing look to annoy her, '*see I told you they were gay,*' even though I didn't believe it for a moment. He continued, "Dom earned a fortune in the City broking, and now a group of them invest in technology projects. He's really smart, more front than most seaside towns, but underneath that, he's one of the good guys."

I was right they were clearly some horrible 'get rich quick' plonkers, part of Maggie Thatcher's capitalist dream. '*Another Martin I bet,*' I thought savagely.

"Wow." said Pen, pushing back a strand of hair that was curling wildly in the steam, and frowned me down.

"What do you do?" I asked.

"I'm the poor relation, just getting my own freelance Consultancy off the ground. Worked Corporate after finishing Uni. for nearly ten years, I had a... a break for a year and decided not to go back."

Something about the slight hesitation before he chose the word 'break' and a slight clouding of his eyes made me curious, it's a professional deformity, reading between the lines and listening for the unspoken. I wondered, what was it, alcohol, drugs, a nervous breakdown.

"I think it’s ready." Said Pen, "Angus can you carve for me please? Everyone OK if I put it straight on the plates?"

And that was how it was at Pen's, mismatched plates, all lovingly collected from jumble sales and charity shops, stacked with delicious homemade, often homegrown, food. There was no ceremony and the warmest welcome you would find anywhere.

Watching everyone round the table relax and let the rich flavours of the roast dinner seduce them, the chat and the laughter took me back to the flat in Sydney...

5. Meeting Brett.

Watching Mark swirl his wine lazily around the glass, his long fingers just lightly balancing the stem, reminded me of Brett, who did exactly the same when he was listening. My mind wandered away from Pen's kitchen and I thought about the day I met Brett.

Temporarily housed in the nurses' quarters at Auburn Hospital in the Western Suburbs, I'd been looking for accommodation to share. I found something promising and rang for an appointment to visit. The following Saturday, I found my way across town to view it. Straightening my hair and making sure my skirt wasn't tucked into my knickers or anything disastrous, I knocked at the door and heard a slightly muffled 'Come in.' I pushed the door and there he was.

Tall and lean with broad shoulders, big hands and the same slim fingers as Mark, Brett was leaning casually against the corner of the kitchen units, polishing off the pickings from a roast chicken carcass. It was sandwiched between two thick slices of loaf and he had a mouthful. He swallowed and with a rueful grin, wiped his greasy fingers on a napkin, extended a hand and said "G'day, I'm being a pig, the chook was just too good. You must be Ellie."

As we shook hands his tan was in stark contrast to my pale English skin.

"Brett?" I queried, "I've come about the flat share, your friend Daniel over at Auburn said you were looking for someone."

"Sure! I'm glad you found it alright. I'll show you around, come on. It's just a small room, but not expensive, and the garden of the flats goes down to the Harbour. It's why I moved in," he explained with a burst of enthusiasm. "I've got a small dinghy, I can sail it right up to the garden wall. Do you sail?"

I felt a swell of queasiness as I remembered the seasickness that overwhelms me on boats and replied "Um... No not really."

The flat was on the first floor of a small three-story block, painted creamy yellow outside and with a beautiful Frangipani tree by the entrance. Inside was simple; white walls, with oversize photos of bush flowers, some of Brett's work, I later discovered. The flat was airy, and open plan, perfect for socialising. A small balcony looked out over the garden and from it I could see a swimming pool, glinting turquoise in the sun. The bedrooms and bathroom were off a short corridor, and Brett was right, the bedroom that would be mine was tiny – a single bed, desk and some fitted cupboards left just about space to turn around.

I didn't care about the room size though, the flat was just what I needed, not expensive and offered guaranteed company whilst I got settled. I'd be out a lot at clinics and studying anyway. Plus, I had only brought to Australia what I could carry on the plane, so I didn't need acres of space.

The biggest room in the flat belonged to Annie and Max. Friends from the neighbourhood they grew up in, Max and Brett had been through school together and were as close to family as you get, without actually being family. He showed me a photo of Annie, who was little and lovely with a mane of blonde hair and golden skin. She was a serious runner he said, and I liked the way he sounded so proud of her. Brett's room was floor to ceiling book shelves. Which endeared him to me immediately, being a bit of a bookworm myself. I noticed some great novels, tomes about photography and a stack of Physio books. Books were interspersed with cameras, lenses and certificates in frames. On the wall above the bed was a black and white poster of Humphrey Bogart in Casablanca. Brett could quote virtually every line, I wasn't quite that good, but it was one of my favourite films, which sealed the deal! We were instant friends.

"If you're interested in the room, you could grab a coffee with me and wait for the others. They said they'd be back soon. Providing they're happy about it, you could move in at the weekend."

Brett moved into the galley kitchen and I sat up on a high stool. He had his back to me and the tartan shirt he had on over a white tee, hung in loose folds as he moved around the kitchen, his forearms bare under the rolled-up sleeves. His hair curled over his collar and I could feel myself falling for him then and there. I told myself it would be better not to take the room if I fancied one of my flatmates, but who was I kidding? I loved the flat. Refusing it on a point of principle seemed daft, I figured that living with him would quickly cure me of any crush I might have.

Whilst we waited, we chatted easily together.

“I finished the Masters course you’ve come to do, two years ago – it’s tough but good.”
“That’s a coincidence, I didn’t realise you were a Physio, if you’ve already done the course, I’ll be able to come to you for help when I get stuck... Where do you work now?”
“In a big practice in the city. One of the Tutors from the course offered me a job. I’ll do a few years, then maybe set up on my own or maybe just go off and travel.”
“What about Annie and Max?”
“Annie’s a PA in the city, no doubt she rules her boss with a rod of iron, and I bet he has no idea. She and Max are together, he’s a junior doctor, works mad hours but he’s very good at his job, so I reckon he’ll get a registrar's job before long.
“Have they been together long?”
“’Bout two years or so, Annie came into the emergency unit with a badly sprained ankle from a running race. Max was on duty at the time and fell for her hook line and sinker. He tries to tell people how she 'fell' for him. But in reality, it was the other way around I’ve known him for ever and she blew him away.”
Before I could ask any more, they came in, in a jumble of shopping bags, fresh flowers and the weekend papers, I felt as if I knew them already from Brett's vivid descriptions. We all seemed to hit it off and I moved my two bags in that weekend.
The rest, as they say, is history and things are now very different. Life can turn on a sixpence. Back then, if you'd told me that four years later, I would be single, with a growing Physiotherapy clinic in Essex, and that Brett would be dead, I would not have believed you. When Brett died, I looked into the abyss, and for a time, longed to step in, to

follow him, but found from somewhere a spark of determination to survive.

As a crash from the cooker brought me back into the moment with a start. I noticed Mark watching me with dark, serious eyes, and wondered how long I'd been wool gathering. Mark's eyes warmed as I caught his gaze and gave him a quick smile. Something of my thoughts must have played across my face because he said "Penny for them."

Nosey blighter, well I was certainly not telling him my private thoughts, "Sorry, I'm not being great company - I was thinking about the Clinic starting tomorrow."

"No, I should apologise," he replied, clearly not believing me, "I'm being nosey, I didn't mean to pry."

The awkward moment was broken by the arrival of a huge rhubarb crumble and for the rest of the evening I made sure I stayed in the moment and enjoyed the company. But he had given me pause for thought, his hesitation about his year off and his quick pick-up on my mood change, didn't quite fit with my brash, city boy judgement. I wasn't letting him off that quickly though there was still the flashy car and the clean wellies, you couldn't trust a man with clean wellies.

6. Trish's story.

Arriving well before time, for my first morning in the new premises, I fumbled with my keys and went to unlock the door. It was already slightly ajar. Rose was there before me.

"Kettle's hot," she called from the kitchen "fancy a cuppa?"

"Yes please. It's still cold out there - roll on the Spring." I settled the two dogs on their beds in my office, clipping the child gate across to stop them welcoming everyone with their usual gay abandon.

Rose appeared from the kitchen carrying two steaming mugs of tea, "Excited?"

"Yes, I am, we've done it Rose, finally, our own premises."

" Well you've worked hard enough Ellie, you deserve it. Goodness knows you haven't had it easy, what with your loss and all. My Jem was just saying the other night 'that girl's got guts' and you know him he doesn't say anything about anything usually."

I was quite overcome, Rose wasn't normally given to empathy and compliments, she was more of a 'get on with it and don't make a fuss.' person. I planted a big kiss on her cheek, to which she replied "Get on with you, Ellie Rose."

Running my finger down the list in the diary, I knew everyone there except Miss Patricia Winter age seventy-five a New Patient. Looking over my shoulder Rose said, "Her Sister booked her in just before we moved. You know her: Kate Walsh from Home Farm. You treated her Husband, Rob, a couple of years ago."

"Yes, I remember, his shoulder kept dislocating, he had to have a surgical repair and was expecting to go out with the cattle the day he got home!"

"That's him."

The first few appointments of the day went without incident, everyone found us and it was lovely to hear all the positive comments about the new premises. Then it was Trish's turn...

Physiotherapy without touch is like Psychiatry without words. I don't know who said that, but it could have been me. I never felt it more keenly than today, as Trish followed me into the treatment room. Blotchy patches across her chest and restless, flicking eyes showed how anxious she was. Her limp on a slightly flexed knee indicated how much pain she was in and her opening gambit, "I don't believe in Physio's, my Sister made me come!" gave me some insight into her personality.

"Do you think she is fussing?" I asked, "Perhaps you could tell me a bit about why your sister is worried."

A triumphant gleam came into her eyes as she responded "It's your job to find out. That's what I'm paying for. If you know what you're doing that is."

Behind all the bluster, I could sense fear and it was my job to find a way to relate to everyone, not just the people that make life easy.

"Well Trish," I replied, after a moment's thought, "to get the best results we need to work as a team. You're right, I'll examine you and hopefully find the root of the problem, but, what you tell me will also help me make choices which speed things up. Shall we see how we get on, then if you think I'm on the right track, we can work together. If you don't think I'm the therapist for you, it won't be a problem."

I paused and fell silent, leaving the ball in her court, the silence stretched on, as she wrestled with herself...

"Oh, go on then," she grunted "I'm here now."

"Excellent, just a couple of questions to make sure it's safe for you to have treatment, then I'll take a look. Tell me where your symptoms are first of all."

"Down the side of my leg to my knee and the knee throbs on both sides, I can't get my weight on it properly and I can't get about. I've got chickens and pigs to look after and no-one to do it for me."

"That must be worrying for you. Does it give way?" I asked, "or get locked and then release with a click?"

"No." She shook her head.

"Have you had a fall or injured it?" I checked.

Something in the downward flick of her eyes told me I may have hit on something, but again she flatly denied it.

I made a note to myself that she may have had a fall, and may need an x-ray, but why would she lie about falling? Domestic violence, fear of losing her independence, pride possibly...

There are red flags which alert therapists to possible problems that are unsuitable for some or all Physio treatments.

I needed to know from Trish about symptoms which could suggest an underlying infection, inflammatory condition or cancer. This involved questions about general health, how her pain behaved during the day and at night, had she had any unexplained weight loss and some family history. I also needed her to gauge a pain score - how bad the pain became on a scale of 0-10 and how easily the pain was provoked. I checked whether she had any loss of feeling or odd sensations like pins and needles. As her symptoms were in the leg, they could be from local tissues or referred through the nerves from the back. Bladder and bowel function can be affected too if the nerves from the sacrum (the triangular bone at the base of the spine) are compressed and cause problems that are a medical emergency, but Trish hadn't had any of those issues.

As none of her replies gave me cause for concern, I decided to glean further information from my reluctant patient by chatting as we went along, rather than completing the interview all in one go. I sensed she was getting restless and wanted to keep her onside.

"Shall we have a look now? I'd like you to take your outer clothes off, down to your underwear, so I can examine your spine and legs." I offered her an open back robe if she felt more comfortable covered but she countered with,

"I expect you've seen it all before."

I watched discreetly as she undressed and noticed how much trouble she had bending and my suspicions grew about her back being part of the problem.

"Lovely, now you're ready could you stand with your feet hip width apart, back to me."

Observing all the while, I noticed how her pained expression increased, as I asked her to straighten the flexed right knee.

She breathed in sharply, “That sends it straight down the side of my leg.”

When I asked her to bend forwards the harmonious curve of the spine was absent, so, instead of forming a smooth curve, like a piece of bent hosepipe, Trish's low back was an unyielding straight line. What movement there was came from the hips and upper back, the low back stayed flat with tight muscles either side splinting it straight. Trish struggled to straighten up again too, managing by taking weight in her arms and walking her hands up her thighs. Side bending was easy to the Left but on the painful Right side, it hurt and she said it sent pain shooting down the leg. Squatting did not seem to present a problem for the knee until Trish got low and her back had to bend as well.

I had seen enough relevant signs during Trish's movements to assess the effect of my *treatment* at the end of the session, so decided I could safely refine the examination at a later date. I was keen to start my *hands-on* assessment now to get a feel for her tissues.

"Would you pop up onto the couch now, lying on your back first please."

I made her comfortable with a pillow under her knees and went to sit at her feet on my stool. Taking a steady breath, I placed my feet firmly on the ground. I asked Trish's permission to use massage oil, checked she had no skin allergies and then warmed some oil in my palms. I placed my hands around her feet, but even before they touched her, I could feel a tired, angry, energy coming off her in a wave. For a moment, I held both feet gently, letting her become accustomed to my touch and feeling Trish's tissues under my relaxed hands. With a firm but light touch, I moved over her skin, moulding the contours of the foot, around the ankle and over the calf, then on up the thigh. As I moved up Trish's painful leg, I felt tight, dry skin with thickened, congested areas all along the side of the leg between the skin and muscle with a reluctance of the knee cap to glide inwards.

"Sore?" I questioned as I returned over the thickened areas. Trish nodded, "been sore for a while?" Trish just grunted. As I worked, I visualised how touch triggers flashes of electrical messaging which speeds along nerves and illuminates reactions in our brains, communication between my hands and her body.

Those areas of thickening did not feel newly formed to me, it takes time for tissues to become leathery like that and there was no increased heat around them, which is often present with a recent injury. I wondered how long had Trish been battling on with this problem alone and why?

Allowing my hands to *melt* through the skin and fascia I began to work over the deeper muscles. Again, I could feel taut bands where I should only find relaxed muscle. Pressure on the tight areas made Trish wince slightly, the tension in her muscles told its tale of repetitive overuse and stress.

I continued on checking her back and legs looking at her pain areas and also any other structures which could be referring into or influencing Trish's pain until I felt I had enough information to safely start treatment.

I began treatment with a light massage, first using long strokes, moulded to the contour of the leg, then a gentle, knead and circle action with my hands from her feet along her legs. Next, I moved along her spine and over her shoulders, keeping a sweeping, firm contact with her skin.

As I worked, I felt Trish's tension begin to melt away, her breathing slowed and her body became heavy on the couch. Hoorah! She was finally relaxing, and the fledgling beginnings of trust were appearing. Under my hands was a wealth of information about Trish's body and because she had begun to realise that beyond any information she gave me verbally, I could feel problem areas and relate what I felt to her daily concerns, Trish began to unbend towards me a little. She was still wary, but I felt we had the start of a working partnership.

"Trish, I think there are two parts to this problem. Your back is at the centre of it all, around where the nerves to your knee come from. Also, your knee cap has got stiff and bound down with very tight soft tissues all down your leg. I think your Sister was right, you did need to come. Judging by the changes in your tissues, I think you've been struggling for a long time.

"Could it be bone cancer? My Mother died of bone cancer." She half whispered her concern.

"No, I don't think so," I replied truthfully "it's more of a mechanical problem."

I explained that stiffness in her spine had caused irritation to the nerves of the leg, which in turn had set off spasm in the muscles and her referred pain. The knee was contributing too, but less. The knee cap depends on an even balance of muscles each side of it, to allow it to run in its groove correctly and hers was being pulled off-centre by over-tight muscles in her leg.

"Is that why I get sharp pains under my knee cap?" She asked

"Yes, it could be. Because the knee cap is pulled sideways by your tight muscles, pressure underneath it is uneven, causing overload in patches which can cause pain and make the knee give way under you. All of which makes you more likely to fall."

“I haven’t said I fall!”

I suspected she did fall sometimes, but let it go “This may not be a perfect knee, there may be some wear and tear changes in the joint, but I think we can make you more comfortable and stronger, with better balance, despite that. I hope that will reduce the risk of you falling in the future too. But for now, I suggest we prioritise treatment for your back to reduce the pain you’re getting, then add in whatever treatment you need on your knee as we progress.”

Trish's careworn face softened just slightly and she gave me a terse nod, "If it isn't cancer, let's see what you can do."

At the reception desk, Rose mouthed "Tricky?" and I scrunched my nose, head on one side considering, then shook my head.

"No, fine."

As Trish left, Rose produced this week’s copy of the local free magazine.

“Look!” she said.

I looked, expecting to see my quarter page advert with its editorial on the new premises and a special offer. However, she showed me a double-page, colour spread with a smiling photo of Martin, photos of his clinic and an article entitled Essex’s Leading Physiotherapy Clinic and a large banner which said *Free Assessment – Call Today*. With the strap line, *Don’t accept the rest, see the best*.

Rose sniffed, “Vulgar and spiteful! Horrible man, why can’t he leave you alone?”

Feigning unconcern, I said, “Rise above it Rose, I refuse to let him spoil our first day.” It wasn’t the first and wouldn’t be the last barb he planted in my flesh.

7. Getting to know Mark.

As February finally released us from its chilly clutches and we headed through March, the temperatures rose a little, and the days drew out. Spring meant Kennel Club Field Training Days for my Setters and Pen's Pointers, so we started to get the dogs fit to go up on the moors and stepped up our obedience training. We both wanted to pass Gundog Working Certificate Tests with our dogs this year and were hoping against hope that someone might invite us to join a Gamekeeper's counting team, if the dogs did well. We both wanted to do some useful work with the dogs. Regular training sessions on the farm fields took on a more determined sense of purpose.

Coming and going from the farm meant I saw Mark and Dom a fair bit. The barn conversion was taking shape, Dom was away on business a lot of the time, mainly there at weekends, but Mark had taken up residence in a mobile home on the site to oversee the building work. They were both regular visitors to Pen and Angus over the couple of months we'd known them.

Angus enjoyed their company, he often worked alone on the farm and he loved having some guys to talk to. Dom could talk a donkey's hind leg off, mainly about himself, sport and had a fund of funny work stories. Mark was different, shy, but once I got to know him, I noticed he had a wry sense of humour and was very kind. He was comfortable to be with when he was on good form, but sometimes seemed abstracted and distant so I wasn't always sure where I stood with him. Dom, was good fun but always had a bit of a glint in his eye, he was fun to flirt with, but a little bit dangerous in the broken heart department I suspected. I enjoyed being part of a group of friends again and we had a lot of fun playing cards for pennies, scrabble, and sharing a bottle of wine at our headquarters in Pen's kitchen.

Only Dom had any spare cash, Mark and I were developing our businesses and Pen and Angus seemed to have land and food but not much positive cashflow. There was always something that needed repairing or replacing on the farm.

Dom brought several girlfriends, never serious, quite sophisticated, and I wondered what they thought of the rest of us. When one particularly stunning blonde with peaches and cream skin who managed to look a million dollars in jeans and a baggy sweater had left, ushered out by the ever-gallant Dom, Pen groaned and said "I feel fat and frumpy, doesn't Dom ever date anyone normal?"

"'Fraid not," said Mark, "ever since school he's always punched above his weight, I don't know how he convinces them he's Robert Redford."

"Anyway, you are not fat and frumpy!" said Angus. "All Dom's girls look as though they need a good meal inside them to me."

Mark shook his head, "None of them last long either, they all just seem like cardboard cut-outs, I'd rather he had someone a bit lower maintenance that cared about him more. Underneath all the front, he isn't a player at all."

"Well, my two champions," said Pen "for that outstanding display of loyalty, I shall treat you to a taster of my world-renowned sloe gin!"

"Oooph, count me out" I said, "I can't face the hangover - be warned Mark, you never have just one! I'm going to hit the trail, I'll see you tomorrow with the dogs, Pen."

"Lightweight!" she said, as I collected my belongings and kissed everyone goodbye.

Crisp and beautiful, the next morning dawned with the promise of a clear day. The grass in the garden was frosty underfoot and I was looking forward to training the dogs. They loaded into the car with their customary enthusiasm. Pen was looking less than her usual bright self when I drew up and walked down to the kennels.

"Good decision to leave early Ellie. I had way too much sloe gin last night - I'm feeling a bit the worse for wear this morning."

"Oh no!" Unable to stop myself laughing, I said "hoist by your own petard, you normally only ensnare unsuspecting guests."

"I know, Mark only had the one and then left. He's got someone to do with the barn coming early this morning. It was Angus and I, we got chatting and had another, and another and put the world to rights. It was lovely, but I'm regretting it today, although he did agree to getting someone in to renovate that horrible upstairs bathroom."

"Goodness, you must have plied him with drink. Well done you. Look, if you're rough, would you rather not come training?"

"Um... Would you mind? It would probably do me good to get out in the fresh air, but I just feel like hugging a pot of coffee and keeping my head still."

"No, its fine, do you mind if I still go?"

"Carry on, walk out towards the Old Farm House and work back across the big fields."

"Thanks. I'll check in on you when I've finished."

A light wind stirred the back of my hair. Bird and Jeeves walked on leads with dancing, impatient steps and only the rustle of my coat and the hollow sound of my Wellies disturbed the peace. Behind us lay a trail of dark green footprints in the frosted grass and our breath rose in condensed clouds. Nearing the far boundary of the farm, I could see the back of Mark and Dom's barn. On the first-floor scaffolding Mark and the builder were already busy. I watched Mark's curly dark head bent over some plans, then as he glanced up, he saw me and waved.

I waved back and was about to turn to start working the dogs, when he called and beckoned "Come and have a look, Ellie."

I walked across the chase that lead to the Old Farm where Angus's parents lived and pushed open the rough gate that was a makeshift access to the Barn.

"Hi, come and see inside if you have time. You haven't seen it since it was a wreck, have you?"

"No, I'd love to have a look." I tied the dogs to the tow hitch of Mark's car, I didn't trust them with all the building stuff about, one would be bound to knock something over or step on a nail.

I followed Mark into the barn and stopped, staring about me, "Wow!"

All the old rubbish had gone from inside and the beams had been cleaned. The big double doors had been replaced with a large picture window and French doors, giving a stunning view across the fields to the river, where the tips of sails were floating, as if boats were skimming across the fields. A mezzanine formed a ceiling over part of the large room. A builder's ladder made the only access upstairs at present, but I could visualise the staircase as Mark described where it would eventually go.

He swept a proud hand round the space, "There will be three bedrooms up there and a first-floor sitting room, games room, whatever. Then, if you can imagine it, this will be the main sitting room and over here will be a kitchen/dining room and office. Then to the left down here another bedroom/en-suite that will be a guest room.

At present, just a skeleton of timber ribs marked out the rooms and the barn was full of dust. It was nonetheless clear the finished design would be magnificent.

"Mark it's amazing. The whole place has a great feel and it's so light and spacious. What a difference that huge window makes."

"I loved the barn the moment I saw it, and I knew Claire would too, of course I couldn't have afforded it without Dom investing as well, but over time I'll end up buying him out. His heart is in London."

"Claire?" Mark had never mentioned her before and I felt a little stab of disappointment when he mentioned her, which surprized me, what did it matter if he had a partner?

"Claire was my wife. I'm widowed, she had Motor Neurone Disease."

"I am so sorry Mark - that's very hard, I didn't know."

"No one does here, apart from Dom. He has been amazing Ellie, I know he can seem a bit shallow, but he saw me, well both of us through this. Lots of people couldn't cope and dropped away, but he didn't and I don't know how I'd have got through without him."

"You and he have been close since school, haven't you? Good on him for being a friend when you needed him. Claire must've been so young Mark, it doesn't seem fair." I felt some of the anger at the injustice of Brett dying young, bubble up inside me again as we spoke.

"No, there was nothing fair about it, but you can't think like that or you'd go crazy. She was only thirty when she died it all happened so fast. About four years before, she started to have trouble swallowing and things kept going down the wrong way. To begin with we laughed about it and I joked it was because she never stopped talking, even when she was eating. We didn't realise anything was wrong. But then she had trouble speaking, her words came out a bit slurred especially when she was tired. The first time it happened, I was away on business and she sounded a bit drunk on the phone and I teased her about it, but she vowed she hadn't had anything to drink. We started to get worried, saw the Doctor and he sent her straight to the Neurologist. It showed up in the tests he did."

Mark hesitated and I put a hand on his arm.

"Don't, if you don't want to talk about it."

"No, I'm alright, I didn't intend to blurt all this out Ellie, her name just slipped out."

"Its fine, if you want to talk, why don't we just walk out with the dogs, I'm not bothered about working them now." Mark's painful story had taken me right back to losing Brett.

"I don't want to spoil your training session..."

"Don't be daft - come on."

We let the dogs loose and watched them bound joyfully away in front of us.

"Mad pair." I said.

Mark smiled as he watched them go.

"We said all the things that everyone says, you know, about beating the odds and not every case being the same, but in the end, it was very aggressive and within two years she could only communicate with a word pad. As she got weaker, she needed a brace to support her neck and head. But it was the breathing that scared me, she couldn't always clear her throat and felt like she was choking."

"Oh, how horrible and so difficult for you to see her go through it."

"It was awful to be pretty much helpless. My work wasn't very sympathetic either. They paid lip service, but at the same time, they wanted me to be there doing my job. In the end I took a year off to help with the nursing and just to be with her. After she died, I never went back to Corporate work, couldn't face it."

"Good, they sound like complete bastards. So, was that when you started up your business?"

"No, I spent six months feeling cheated and angry. I felt guilty too and ended up not doing much that was constructive. Claire would have been ashamed of me. I lost myself completely and went on a bender, didn't wash or dress some days and drank way too much."

"I'm not surprised."

"It was Dom who picked me up and gave me a shake in the end. He volunteered me to do some consultancy for one of his clients - which was where my business idea came from. I sold our house and with the money from that, life insurance and a bit of investment from Dom, I bought the barn. I needed a project I could lose myself in and some physical labour. I've certainly been sleeping better since I started."

I looked across the fields digesting all he'd said, we had something in common after all, I thought, and his moodiness seemed more justified now. On the far edge of the field, I watched the watery spring sun, glimmer out over two trees, knobbly against the sky where Angus had pollarded their branches to encourage fresh growth. Poor things, did trees feel pain like we did when they were cut back to bare subsistence by? I wondered about changing the subject but the question was out of my mouth before my brain had fully engaged.

"What was she like?" Oh no! what business did I have asking that? He didn't seem to mind, he paused for a moment as if conjuring up her face,

"Well, it's really hard to describe someone, but she was a gentle soul, very blonde with blue eyes and a nice face, not flashy or beautiful in the conventional sense, but very caring and thoughtful which made her beautiful, if you see what I mean?"

I nodded.

"She saw good in everyone and when she was playing with the kids her face just lit up and she was always laughing."

"Oh, you have children?"

"No, not us, although we were going to have a family, she worked with special needs kids at a day care centre."

"She sounds like a lovely person Mark, what a tragedy that she died so young."

"Life isn't fair though is it? I am getting better, things are coming together and I can see a way forward. So, enough about me, what about you? You seem to love your work..."

Relieved to get onto safer ground and wondering if he'd begun to regret opening up, I took the reprieve he'd given me and said, "Mostly I do, I see some real characters that's for sure. I've just recently discharged a lady who didn't want to see me in the first place and definitely didn't tell me all the truth when she first came in!" I was thinking about Trish Winters, "In the end, she and I worked together for about six weeks and credit where it's due, once we got going, she did everything I asked, worked very hard at all the exercises and accepted my advice."

"Doesn't everybody?"

"No! You'd be surprised... By the end she was in great shape, with no pain and finally made a confession that she'd been falling before her treatment, but hadn't told me because she worried she wouldn't be able to stay at home with her animals if the family found out."

The confession when it finally came, had been another piece of the Trish jigsaw in place and confirmed my suspicions.

"On her last session she pushed a carrier bag into my hand, which contained six eggs from her hens, a pot of home-made jam and a fruit cake. She told me I was *alright*. I can't remember when I've had a nicer compliment"

He laughed. "What brought you to Essex?"

So, did I tell a lie? But I thought not, how awful would it be if he found out through Pen the real reason and felt I hadn't trusted him with my confidence, the way he had trusted me with his. I plunged in, "Ah, well actually, I lost someone too, about four years ago now." I swallowed and carried on in a rush, "he wasn't ill like Claire, he died in an accident and you have been braver than me, I am only just getting my head above water now."

" Ellie, I'm so sorry. I've been bashing on for ever, like I'm the only person who ever lost anyone and you've been listening, when you have your own tragedy. I've caught you in unguarded moments looking sad, but assumed it might be a recent break up or something."

" A pair of battle-scarred survivors," I joked. "Seriously though, its fine to talk. I get the anger and despair bit totally, there were times I felt like I wouldn't make it and times I could've destroyed worlds I felt so angry. But here I am four years later and it's better, it really is. Building up the clinic kept me sane, working till I dropped, it got me through too."

We looked at each other and I gave him a wry smile.

"Right!" he said "No more sadness this morning, you deserve a decent coffee and a bacon sandwich, but you won't get one in my caravan. How about we put the dogs in your car, as we're nearly back at Pen's and I'll take you to the cafe at the Marina?"

"I'd like that" I said and genuinely meant it.

8. Headache.

Pen and I returned from our training weekend in the Yorkshire Dales with grins a mile wide and waving certificates! All four dogs had been awarded their Gundog Working Certificates and we were thrilled. Our trainer for the weekend was Mike Neville, we had worked with him before, when Jeeves was a youngster and he'd been incredibly helpful. His Father had bred and worked Pointers, so Mike had grown up with pointing breeds and was that rare commodity, someone able to teach, not just how he would train his dogs, but who could look at you and your dog to see what would work best for your partnership. My big clown Jeeves had progressed and Mike was very pleased with him, but he instantly loved Bird.

"She's a great dog! You could do anything with her - cracking!" I was bursting with pride, Mike wasn't a great one for lavish praise.

After my walk with Mark and our revelations, the weekend away had been very welcome. I felt conflicted about all I'd heard and all I'd confided in return. It was powerful stuff and recently, I'd kept my sadness and grief neatly contained. Was this going to bring it all back and would he want to talk about it all the time? I wasn't sure I could cope and this was not what I'd intended, when I'd made my vow to lighten up. I wasn't sure how I felt about the new turn of events.

When we burst in, full of our weekend in the fresh air and our success, Angus, not missing his cue, got out the champagne. He phoned Mark to join us and I felt embarrassed and awkward as he came in. I wondered how we'd be together. He seemed unphased and made no mention of our conversation, nor any attempt to so much as catch my eye with a meaningful look. I relaxed a bit and we toasted the clever dogs together in Pen's kitchen. A moment of unclouded happiness; it felt good. It seemed so long since I'd felt like this, able to laugh and joke, with everything in focus, not shrouded in a dark veil of grief. But when I got home and started to undress, I felt a paradoxical annoyance. Why hadn't he acknowledged what we'd shared in any way? Suddenly, I was no longer sure if I was relieved or slightly offended. I should lay off the Champagne it clearly addled my brain.

As hawthorn and cherry blossom gave way to new green leaves, and roses appeared in the gardens, the days lengthened and I began little by little to feel more whole again. Mark continued to keep our friendship easy and we grew relaxed in each other's company. We didn't live in each other's pockets, but it was lovely to have someone to do things with. We didn't have physio in common like Brett and I had, but we did chat together, amongst other things, talking over the perils of starting a new business. I watched as his barn conversion took shape, popping in with the dogs to see the latest bit completed and chatting about the next phase. We both liked going to the movies, shared suppers and the odd bit of being each other's 'plus one' when we had an event to attend. Only simple things, but it made a world of difference to me and eased my loneliness. He seemed to need a friend too. Of course, he could be a grumpy old git and annoyed me several times by dropping out of things at the last minute with excuses... "Ellie I'm sorry, I'm tired tonight, do you mind if we don't go out?" The pom pom was when he said "Dom thinks I should try one of those dating agencies, what do you think?"

Think? What did it matter what I thought? "Do what you like," I replied then changed the subject.

The clinic seemed to be going fairly well, I didn't want to jinx anything, but I was getting steadily busier. The trouble was, busier meant working longer hours. Pen reminded me, nearly as often as she nagged me about getting a boyfriend, "You can't maintain this pace for ever girl, you'll make yourself ill. Something's going to give!" It was a conundrum; I wasn't sure I could afford to take on more staff. Rose was also finding the longer hours onerous, which meant thinking about another receptionist as well as an extra physio. She and I agreed to see how things continued over the Summer and into Autumn when I would have to start thinking seriously about recruiting some help.

Towards the end of June, after a lazy weekend getting the house straight, indulging in some overdue T'ai Chi practice and reading in the garden, I heard the phone ring. I put my book aside and scrambled up from the comfy spot I was in, leaning against the willow tree, to run in and answer it.

"Hi Mark."

"Hi Ellie, I was ringing to see if you would like to go over to Mersea this afternoon? We could walk the dogs and go for some seafood. I've checked the tides and the causeway is clear."

I was surprised, I hadn't seen much of him since the dating agency conversation, I'd been busy and he'd been... well, I supposed, busy going out on dates. I thought about saying no, but then thought it was childish and said instead, "Sounds good, I'm happy to drive. I can pick you up in half an hour or so, I need to brush up a bit," I eyed my tousled reflection and scruffy clothes in the mirror. I also noticed bits of dead leaves forming a collage on the back of my tee shirt. I bet he was used to better from his dating agency girls, I'd show him I scrubbed up nicely too.

"See you soon," he said and clicked the phone down.

I whizzed up the ladder stairs to my bedroom and dragged a brush painfully through the knots in my hair. Gathering it into a pony tail, I gave a twist and secured it up in a makeshift chignon, releasing a few tendrils around my face. I shed my garden clothes on the floor and pulled on some dark brown linen trousers and a sleeveless, amber silk shirt. Sensible enough to walk the dogs in, but a bit smarter than jeans for the restaurant. A quick spritz of Chanel's Cristalle, my favourite summer perfume, citrus, florals and enough woody notes to be intriguing, then I was ready.

The dogs didn't need to be asked twice, they hopped into the crate at the back of the car, full of enthusiasm for whatever we were doing.

Mark was perched on the wall at the front of the barn as I drew up, ankles crossed, a jumper slung round his shoulders with the arms tied loosely in front. His white tee shirt showed off his olive skin. He looked less tired, more relaxed than he had earlier in the year and it suited him.

"Hi Ellie," he dropped a bag on the back seat and lent across to give me a kiss on the cheek as he got in the car, "you smell nice."

I had been thinking the same about him and felt slightly embarrassed to find I enjoyed his casual kiss so much.

“Well thank you. What's in the bag?"

"It's for later," he teased "you'll see..."

"Oooh, mysterious."

Tails drumming against the side of the crate indicated Jeeves and Bird were pleased to see Mark too. He turned and said

“Hi dogs!” which increased the tattoo to fever pitch before we set off through the country lanes via Hatfield Peveral then headed East along the A12, turning off for Mersea Island after Colchester.

“So, how’s the dating been going?”

“Dating?” He looked confused for a second, then said “The online stuff? Um, well I only did one date. She was nice enough, but I don’t think it’s for me, the whole blind date thing. Dom says I’m hopeless.”

“You are not hopeless,” I fired up, “tell Dom to mind his own business.”

We parked up at Cudmore Grove Park and ambled along the trails to the beach, Bird and Jeeves darting from side to side in front of us, delighted to be somewhere different with new smells. They had great fun in and out of the water too, chasing stones that Mark had the knack of skimming across the surface.

"I thought we'd try The Company Shed to eat," said Mark dusting off his hands on his trousers.

“I haven’t heard of that one.”

"You can't book, so we may have to queue. They sell fabulous seafood apparently, it hasn't been open long.”

“I thought maybe you’d brought us a picnic in the bag...”

“Well not quite, it’s some bread, lemon wedges, implements various and a bottle of wine, hopefully still cold. They don't serve any of the extras it’s a no-frills kind of a place."

I smiled, “Oh so you think I’m a no-frills kind of a girl?”

He looked horrified, then realised I was teasing. How nice it was to be out together again when he was in a good mood.

My lolling tongued dogs were grateful to get back in the car and both managed to get their heads into the large bowl of water, lapping enthusiastically. Jeeves pausing only to give me a wide mouthed, slobber-drooling grin as I closed the door. We relocated to the quayside, found a parking space in the shade and left all the windows and the half door at the back fully open to ventilate the car. It wasn't a particularly hot day but the inside of cars can get dangerously hot very quickly. I don't take any chances with the dogs. The Shed was doing a roaring trade. We decided to buy a selection of seafood at the window and eat it out of the bag, on the harbour wall, rather than wait for a table. The fresh seafood made a picnic fit for kings. Sucking my lemony, salty fingers and wiping them on a napkin I said, "Inspired choice Mark, that was delicious." I shook my head as he offered more wine, "Not when I'm driving thanks."

He stood up, "Ready for home?" I nodded and he reached out his hand and pulled me to my feet.

The journey back was companionable with bursts of conversation and easy silences. Sun-kissed and pleasantly weary, I dropped him at the barn and thanked him for the invitation. As he waved me off and I drove home I thought again how much I’d enjoyed myself. I hadn’t felt so relaxed since I was with Brett. ‘Oh my goodness. Brett, I’m sorry, I’m sorry, I’m sorry, I didn’t mean it, nothing could be as much fun as being with you.' Could he see I wondered? If he could, did it make him sad to see me with Mark? "Stop it"! I said to myself, it was just a day out.

Monday morning came around all too quickly and I pushed the door of the clinic knowing I had a busy day ahead of me. Reception felt cool and a discreet smell of bergamot, lavender and geranium lingered from the massage oils I use. I bent over the desk, scanning today's list. Just one new patient, Louise Maybury, about halfway through the morning, after my break. She was already waiting as I said goodbye to the patient before her, which put paid to my tea break. I didn't mind too much, it's easy to over-run with someone new and it would save me getting behind later on. Her name hadn't rung a bell, but as soon a she looked up, I remembered her, my patient from Martin's clinic, the day we had fallen out and he'd fired me.

"Hi Louise, come on in." I smiled in welcome and gestured her into the treatment room. "Do sit down, what brings you today?"

"Hi Ellie, I'm so glad I've found you again, I'm sure he's a very good therapist but I couldn't get on with Martin, he made me feel stupid." she replied with a sigh that carried a sad note of exhaustion and defeat.

Tall and slender with a stooped posture, she reminded me of a broken reed. Her face was sallow with dull black shadows under her eyes and a weary resigned expression, yet she was very elegantly dressed in matching coordinates and expensive shoes.

"I have terrible headaches, I've had them for years, at least two or three a week. Sometimes I wake at night with them, other times they build up as the day goes on."

I said nothing about Martin, but my blood boiled, his patronising attitude was the last thing she needed. "Can you show me where you feel the headaches?"

She pointed to the area at the top of her neck just under the skull on her hairline, then indicated a sweep over her head to her left eye.

"Sometimes it feels like my head is in a vice and that someone is pushing my eye out from behind the socket. It's weird too because my ear can feel full as if it's blocked too."

"Have you had any investigations for this at all?"

"I've been everywhere! Doctor, Specialist, had a brain scan, blood tests and everything comes up normal. I'm sick of taking painkillers that do nothing and it's really getting me down."

"Sounds horrible, I'm not surprised it's getting you down. Can I ask what painkillers you were prescribed?"

"Over the years, Paracetamol, Codeine, Tramadol, some anti-epileptic that made me feel like a zombie... none of it works." Out of the blue, tears welled up and rolled down her cheeks which she dashed away, "Sorry I didn't mean to cry, I feel at the end of my tether."

Louise told me about her busy job in London as a PA, typing under time pressure and often on the phone with the receiver tucked under her left ear as she wrote messages. Her work station had a word processor which she swivelled to use and she sat on a standard office chair with only height adjustment. Outside work she was pretty tired, so tended to grab a quick meal and collapse on the sofa on weekday evenings. She had good intentions of exercising but didn't make it regularly and played the violin for her own pleasure.

"Do you ever feel sick with the headache or get numbness in your lips or tongue?" She shook her head, "Or get flashing lights or a halo round your eye when the headache comes?"

"No, I don't. The Consultant asked all that, because I thought I had migraines, but he said no."

"Shall we have a look?" I invited her to sit on the couch.

Bearing in mind what she'd told me, I guided her through a series of tests, watched her move and put my hands on to feel for tight tissues and areas of stiffness that might be contributing to her problem. As I moved through the examination, a pattern began to emerge that I explained.

"I think I can see what may be causing your headaches Louise, it seems to be a combination of your posture..."

She cut in, "I know it's terrible, I hated being tall at school so I slouched, my Mum was always telling me to stand up straight."

"Some of things you do regularly, as well as the posture, contribute to your headaches, because they make you compress the upper joints of your neck. Tilting your neck or looking to the left, like when the phone is tucked under your ear or when you play your violin, does the same thing. Constantly being compressed makes joints hurt. Over time, your muscles adapt to the compressed position and become short and tight. Then, Trigger points in those tight muscles refer pain too."

"What, right over my head to the eye? As severe as I'm getting it?"

"Well yes, because the nerves from the top of your neck supply the skin and muscles of the scalp and they also join onto some of the cranial nerves which are involved with the function of your eyes and ears. Nerve tissue is like a continuous branching tree, from the root ball in the brain to the tiny branches at the tips of your toes and fingers, all nerves are connected. Irritation of the nerves at the top of your neck could account for the odd feelings you're having, like the full ear and your eye being pushed forward. They come from your brain trying to make sense of the faulty nerve signals and coming up with an explanation it can imagine."

"Oh, I see, I didn't realise that could happen."

"When you sit slouched, your head ends up about three inches in front of the spine. If you imagine your head weighs about ten to twelve pounds, in that position, the weight of it isn't being supported by the bony architecture of the spine, so the ligaments and muscles are straining to hold it up, a bit like a large lollipop bending its stick."

"I didn't realise that headaches can be referred from the neck."

"Lots of headaches are. The good news is, most of what we've talked about is reversible. I can help you re-learn a more economical posture, strengthen your muscles and also do some manual therapy and stretching to speed up the process."

"I'm happy to try anything."

"For today, I'm going to give you some information about setting your work station up correctly and I'd like you to spend some time rearranging your desk. It would help a lot to bring more movement into your day too. Walk the long route to the toilets, get away from your desk for a walk at lunchtime and change position every half an hour or so at work. I'll teach you how to stretch your neck and shoulders."

Confident a course of treatment would be helpful, I was looking forward to working with her.

Louise's follow up appointment seemed to come around incredibly quickly. I couldn't believe a week had flown by since we'd been together learning stretches and discussing work station layouts. She had been busy with the information I'd given her and already, she reported her headaches were less severe and coming on later in the day. Louise had also tackled her boss and he had agreed to order a better office chair that was more adjustable.

Posture correction work was a treatment priority, but it turned out, to be difficult. Louise struggled to feel where her head and shoulders should be. Her joint position sense or proprioception wasn't good and I made a mental note that this may slow her progress down. Sadly, where posture is concerned the brain doesn't have much quality control, it simply repeats the patterns of movement we use most frequently as it’s default mode. We needed to rewrite Louise's body programme to make the corrected posture become her "normal" and that meant lots of repetition over the next six weeks.

"I can't believe I can't do this," she wailed as, unless I helped her, she floundered to find the right position for her neck and shoulders.

"Well if it was easy, I guess we'd all be doing it with no help. Don’t worry you’ll get there.”

To help, we worked using a mirror and also used some of the new adhesive sports tape, to remind her what she was aiming for. The tape applied in the corrected postural position, stretched if she slouched. Louise could feel the stretch on her skin, alerting her to correct her posture. The extra feedback seemed to help and by the end of the session, I felt confident that with the extra cues it gave her, she would be able to practice successfully on her own.

"Everything feels lighter with the tape on," she said "my shoulders aren't dragging on my neck now."

As Louise left, I gave her some red sticky dots to put around the office and at home as visual reminders to do her posture correction even when she was busy.

When she came back the following week, she reported that her pain levels were down to three out of ten not the eight out of ten we had started with. I checked her exercises, which were going well, but not ready to be progressed yet.

"Today you get to chill out and let me do some of the work. Everything we are doing is putting credits in your body's bank account, so we are gradually paying off the overdraft and trying to get you back in the black. I'm going to do some hands- on work today to try to speed things up for you."

The mobilisation and myofascial release techniques I used during that session, gently restored some of the lost movement in the upper part of her back and neck which made it easier for her to hold her new posture.

Chatting to Mark, Pen and Angus about my week, when we met up for a drink on Friday, I was explaining about posture and headaches. Mark guiltily sat up straighter in his seat and Pen laughed.

"Posture Police," she teased "Physios have that effect on people. Shame they don't practice what they preach about work/life balance though; Ellie Rose, workaholic."

She had a point. "You're right, Pen, I know you're right" I conceded. I had done nothing about lightening up. Working hard with others was maybe just a great way to avoid confronting my own issues, I thought guiltily.

My guilt didn't stop me being excited to see Louise the following week especially when she arrived with a big smile.

"No headaches for four days!" she said doing a little happy dance.

"Brilliant!"

We got down to work adding in some mat work exercises that challenged her postural muscles more. To give her confidence, we also prepared some of the exercises that might come up if she joined an exercise class.

“I think I’d better hide at the back of the class” she laughed as she tried to lift one arm up from an all fours table position and wobbled perilously, completely losing her upper body position.

“Maybe a couple more individual lessons before we let you loose on the world!”

With stress factors high for her at work, I taught Louise some simple relaxation techniques and suggested she might prefer Yoga or T'ai Chi classes to a gym-based class. Both would include posture, exercise and relaxation. At least I did both regularly, I hoped that might be my ‘get out of jail’ card when it came to overworking. I certainly didn’t want to end up with the headaches Louise had, nor any of the other stress related problems like high blood pressure or ulcers. Pen was right I needed to back off and lighten up a bit.

As she lay down on the couch under a soft blanket, I dimmed the light and put some gentle music on in preparation for the relaxation session. She sighed contentedly “Yes, I much prefer this to doing exercises.” I think we both benefitted from those ten minutes breathing and relaxing.

We finished our work together earlier than I'd expected, as Louise became completely pain free. Many patients who lead busy lives, come back from time to time when good intentions slipped in the face of life happening. I suspected

Louise may be one of those, clearly the same thought had crossed her mind too,

"Ellie, I'm really worried that if I stop seeing you, it will all come back," she said when I suggested I could discharge her.

"Think of me as one of the tools in your toolbox, if you think you need help, you know where I am, but I'm confident you'll manage fine most of the time."

Working with people is not all beer and skittles but when everything goes according to plan it gave me a fantastic feeling of satisfaction.

9. Flashback to Japan.

As I arrived at the clinic the following week, Rose handed me a small pile of bills and a letter.

Money was not as tight as it had been at the start, but I still felt anxious as we headed through the first year in the new premises, that making the business loan repayments could be a problem, if we had a quiet patch. I still needed to be cautious about spending. Bills always made my stomach lurch, so I put them aside on my desk, and concentrated on the letter, I'd look at them later.

It came from the Acupuncture Association advertising the upcoming conference and reminded me I needed to do some continuing professional development in order to retain my membership. I hadn't had the time or the money before the move to do more than read and review some research articles and write up a case history, but a course or a conference to attend would be good.

This year's acupuncture conference was only a couple of months away and looking at the speakers and workshop topics advertised in the letter, I thought the two-day event sounded interesting. I was keen to hear researcher Helen

Langevin presenting new evidence on how acupuncture may work via the fascia, which could impact on the musculoskeletal problems I treat.

Forgetting day to day worries like bills and my love life, I remembered back to my happy student days in Sydney. Brett and I had spent hours discussing articles about Physiotherapy and I loved anything that gave me evidence as to why my preferred hands on techniques worked. There's a substance in the body called fascia which is fascinating stuff, but until recently wasn't much talked about and wasn't well understood. Bones, muscles, ligaments, tendons, organs etc. are fairly familiar parts that make up a body. Because the medical profession gained much of its structural knowledge about the body through dissection of dead bodies, we tend to think of the body as lots of different component parts that are joined up or connected together like Mechano. But there are certain things that don't quite make sense with that theory when you consider a living body. For example; how can there always be the same spaces between the two bones of a joint whether we are standing or lying? By rights, bones should surely be compressed together when we stand? Biotensegrity is a concept that puts forward the theory that the body isn't lots of separate components bolted together, but is one continuous blended structure.

I was discussing this with Bob, a patient who came in to see me regularly, either with back ache or a stiff shoulder. I was trying to convince him to do exercises for his whole body, not just the bit that was hurting at the time without much success. Today's discussion was about his very tight hamstrings and why I thought they could be the trigger for his recurring problems all over the body.

"Come off it, Ellie - what have tight muscles at the back of my legs got to do with my shoulder?"

"Fair question Bob - how long have you got?"

"They aren't joined up or anything are they?"

" Well actually, they are joined up by a substance called fascia"

"What's fascia then?"

"It's a gel like structure that is in and around every tissue in the body, completely continuous, no breaks anywhere. When you cut up meat, you can see it, it's the sticky, pearly looking membrane between the sections of meat. It looks really fragile, but it's amazingly tough and difficult to tear or chop off."

"Yeah, yeah, I know, it gets stuck on your hands and it feels sort of wet and slimy."

"Exactly! The theory is, that fascia (along with other elastic tissues) makes a kind of tension matrix which allows the body to be strong and yet very flexible without ending up with damaging forces anywhere. It bends and deforms as we move, letting us get into some real contortions, but then recoils back to its original shape."

"I wish! My kid has got a bendy, stretchy toy thing that does that."

"I've seen those advertised on the telly, they look brilliant. Well this theory says that the hard parts of our anatomy like the bones, are not so much a lever system operated by pulleys (the muscles) and held together by straps (the ligaments) but rather, bones are suspended within a network of elastic tension. Everything is continuous with everything else, so the body can be springy and supple, yet absorb and distribute load and still stay stable as we move about."

"Blimey, my body hasn't been springy and supple for a long time."

"Yes, I know and that's the whole point of me nagging you to do some more exercise! You can't say the shoulder is the shoulder and the legs are the legs and keep them separate, because research says the Maths is wrong. The body couldn't function as a simple lever biomechanics system. Load has to be redistributed somehow. Otherwise some of the everyday activities we do, like lifting a kettle, would generate enough force on the bones and discs of the spine to cause them to explode."

"You're kidding!"

"No honestly, intra-abdominal pressure, when you pull in your tummy muscles, could offset some of the force on your spine, but even with this, the maths doesn't stack up. Something else is happening to offload the spine and the idea of the body as a tensioned, suspension structure may be closer to the truth."

"That's really interesting, so it's a bit like how a suspension type bridge holds up."

"Yes. If the Biotensegrity idea is right, the simplest movement can cause changes in tension anywhere in the body. What we do in one place, can have an effect somewhere else. If we take a local view, you having tight hamstrings may only mean you're likely to get a hamstring tear, but if this theory is right, the lack of flexibility in your legs could be causing a problem elsewhere in the body by causing overload as a knock-on effect."

"Like pain in my back."

"Yes exactly. But also, as far away as your shoulder, if it causing tension that is offset through the whole body. An easy way to think about it is, if your shirt is tucked in too tightly at the waist, when you go to lift your arm, the tension through the shirt, will stop you, even though there is nothing wrong with your arm. If the hamstrings are tethered, they can't pay out to let the tissues on that side slide up which lets you lift your arm."

"Is that why you treat trigger points all over the place even if the main pain is in my shoulder?"

"Yes. What we do in one place may have a very widespread influence on the body. It certainly may explain why using distant acupuncture points works. You know when your shoulder is bad and I put a needle into the side of your calf which helps with the pain and frees it up?" Bob nodded, "Well we can see on live scans, through an ultrasound microscope, that acupuncture needles lift and tension sheets of that tissue we were talking about - fascia. We also see the needle activate cells around it for many centimetres. It all could be another piece in the jigsaw of how acupuncture works. Acupuncture aside, it could explain how lots of what we do with manual therapy and massage techniques work."

" Yep, I can see why you are always talking about me doing stretches and stuff then."

"Great, so do you think you'll give some stretching a go now?" I asked, thinking I might have a light bulb moment here.

"Nah! I know I should, but I hate doing exercises."

"Oh, Bob honestly..."

"Interesting what you said though, I can understand better, but I'd rather come in and get you to do me a whole-body treatment."

Well you can't win them all! I had to laugh, at least he was honest. Bob made me think with his light-hearted take on life, that maybe I was a bit too intense all the time and maybe I should lighten up on duties and responsibilities a bit too.

I then completely ignored that thought. Just chatting with Bob about all the delicious complexities of the body and how much exciting research is out there, made the decision for me and despite bills and tight funds, I asked Rose if she would book me in for the conference.

To salve my conscience about how much it would cost, I decided to fore-go the gala dinner and all the trimmings and just travel up for the conference days - which would also save on hotel bills. If Brett had been alive, we would have done it all, him laughing and chatting to everyone at the dinner, then twirling me around the dance floor. But he wasn't, alive.

Still, I promised myself that once the conference was done, I was definitely going to lighten up, listen to Pen and get more of a life!

10. Hashima

The last conference I'd attended had been several years before when I was still in Australia and a post grad. student. Brett and I had travelled to Japan. Two days of lectures in, and he was already fidgety. His Physiotherapy brain saturated with conference lectures, the creative photographer in him was bursting to get out.

He began enticing me to play hooky with a ghost story, "Hashima Island, is supposedly one of the ten most haunted places in the world" he tempted, "and only a short boat trip from where we were staying." His photographer's brain was in overdrive and he was desperate to go.

"Aww come on Ellie! It'll be great. Pretty please?" His handsome face looked expectantly into mine, watching for any tiny 'tell' that would show him I was relenting from my previously adamant position of "No! Not in a million years!" I was not going ghost hunting, I continued, "We've already paid for a full Conference day tomorrow."

"We don't have to be at the conference every day, it's not school," he laughed, "you're being a girly swot again!"

I aimed a swipe at his shoulder, but he pulled away laughing. "I sometimes wonder if you are really a Physio in your heart of hearts Brett, or if you should do the photography full time, or even be a journalist." I said.

"Yeah, I know I should probably go to the lectures, but it'd be more fun to play truant and see if this place is really as creepy as they make out!"

He knew he had me, I never was much good at keeping a poker face. He was already tapping in the search details for our trip from the conference centre in Nagasaki to Hashima ten miles to the South.

"How do you do that?" I laughed, landing my punch this time.

"You love me babe!" he replied and it was true.

There was no ferry to the abandoned island, I wasn't convinced we were even supposed to be going. Undeterred, Brett set about finding some transport. After chatting with staff at the hotel, he managed to hire a small fishing boat to take us across, owned by the Brother of one of the kitchen porters.

The little white boat was spotless, but a strong smell of fish assailed my nostrils as we boarded her, rising from the front catch area. Haru-san our captain, showed us to a tiny deck behind the small bridge, where he had thoughtfully draped the old bench with a blanket and sprinkled some cherry blossom.

"Haru mean 'calm sea'," he smiled, "good journey today, romantical." Then laughed delightedly at his gentle joke.

The journey to Hashima took just over an hour and as it was a lovely calm day on the water, the boat trip was a pleasure. As we left the port at Nagasaki, I looked back on the lively, bustling town with its rounded, green hills behind and wondered what the ghostly island would be like. As we forged through the calm sea, the wind dispelled the fishy smell. I leant against Brett, relaxing, with the sun on my face. Around us, sharp points of rocks and small islets pierced the sea like the dorsal fins of sea monsters. I grudgingly acknowledged that this was better than being in stuffy lecture rooms and quite 'romantical'.

As we approached the island, its concrete hulk rose from the water like a gigantic fortress or some science fiction battleship. The sea-wall dwarfed our boat as we approached and the gaunt ruins of the buildings immediately cast a sombre shadow on my mood. Ruined mine chimneys, that had once belched toxic smoke into the air, stood silent, sentinels to this abandoned place.

Brett hitched his camera equipment onto his shoulder in readiness to dis-embarque as we drew alongside an old pier. He stepped out of the boat confidently, as I had seen him step off his own dinghy back home in Sydney, so many times. He turned, smiling and handed me out of the boat. I sprang up onto the rust-stained concrete pier. Blisters of paint peeled from the blue safety railings, to expose the raw metal, and scabs of it lay scattered on the floor beneath, like the confetti from a long-forgotten wedding.

I stepped forward and took in the mass of decaying concrete that loomed ahead of me and felt even more oppressed by the sad carcass of this once thriving industrial town. Over five thousand people had been packed onto this tiny island, many little more than slaves. Brett leaned in to me as I stared and said "Boo!"

"Oh! For Goodness sake! You made me jump out of my skin."

He grinned wolfishly, "are you ready to face the most haunting or haunted, abandoned place on earth?"

"Lead on!" I quipped, feeling slightly less jaunty than I sounded.

As we walked along the pier, I shivered slightly. This place gave me a nasty chilly feeling and I drew my thin cardigan more tightly around me. I glanced back to the sea, I couldn't help wishing our little boat was still tethered there, rather than disappearing back across the blue, towards the mainland.

Catching my glance Brett said, “He’ll be back in a couple of hours.”

Sad reminders of the community that had lived here were everywhere. A bright red children's bike, now dusty and rusting, lay abandoned on its side, the wheel spinning disconsolately, powered only by the onshore breeze, no longer by eager, peddling legs. No laughter rang around the deserted tenements, to brighten their hollow-eyed, curtain-less facades with the colour of joy. Only sad remnants of bags and old cartons flapped disconsolately in the wind.

Brett turned this way and that, snapping the shutter again and again. Placing the camera between himself and the atmosphere like a shield. He chatted words of encouragement to himself: "Excellent!", "Amazing!", "Wow!"

My presence, so desired the day before, was almost forgotten. The intimate relationship between the camera, his eyes and Hashima, blossomed and he lovingly explored its flesh and bones.

But another presence was troubling me, amongst the crumbling concrete, where pioneering grasses thrust their scrubby, green blades skywards and creepers slithered across steps, out of windows and over walls, I felt the envious energy of a young woman following us, curious and longing.

I glanced behind but saw no-one. Yet I could have sworn... a girl with a dirty face and over large eyes, half smiling at Brett. She brought with her the unanswered question "Are you mine?" The question seemed to me to hang in the air and I had to stop myself from saying “No! He’s mine.”

"Can we go back to the sea soon?" I called to Brett, thoroughly spooked "I'm getting chilly."

"Hmm?" Came the distracted reply. Brett had just seen a staircase. Its steps blackened by ingrained coal dust and by design rickety, the staircase snaked its way between two tall buildings with bamboo clad balconies.

"How did they feel, the workers? As they trudged, exhausted up the steps from the mines beneath the sea, towards their homes. Was there any joy in their lives here?" Or had the steps mainly been a downward stairway to hell, path to the airless and dust laden mines. Dust that burdened the lungs of healthy men, until they became thin shadows, skin tattooed in black like a pen and ink sketch?

And there she was again, in the periphery of my vision, always just out of sight, a wisp of a hint of a girl, watching Brett, waiting.

I was letting my imagination run away with me, I disliked this deserted, sad place and my mind was playing tricks. Brett saw Hashima through artists eyes and for him, it was a place of fascinating angles, brooding shadow and light play. I felt differently, I could sense a cold, repressed energy here, a longing for life. However, as I watched him work, I saw his enthusiasm and when he had the shots he needed, I hugged him to me, reassuring myself. He was warm, strong and alive. For a moment irrationally, I became terrified I would lose him.

“Hey, Babe,’ he said softly, brushing a tendril of hair that the wind had blown across my face, “shall we take some fun shots?”

I shook off the creepy feeling I’d had, and we played in the sun, shooting a series of fast-shutter speed shots of me disappearing through doorways. The tantalising glimpse of my half-turned body or the edge of my skirt, blown back by the breeze, showing on the photos. Our laughter was vibrant against the muted quiet of the town and my movement a juxtaposition to the stillness. As I looked back over my shoulder laughing into the camera, trailing my cardigan behind me, I froze; in the halo of the sun, behind his head, I saw her, standing right behind him, but then he moved and there was nothing there.

Photos finished, we wandered back to the pier and I was grateful to lounge in the sun, eating our picnic; forebodings gone, normality restored, whilst we waited for the boat to return.

My favourite photo of that day was a time-lapse portrait of the two of us down on the pier, laughing into the camera, frozen in time, forever happy in our togetherness. I had not known then, as Haru-San docked the boat and we finally boarded to leave the dead town, that the photos of Hashima were to be the last Brett took. He, like the community from the town and the girl, would soon be gone; leaving behind only a shadow, a hint of his presence carried in my heart.

The memory felt like a cold hand over my heart and it took me the rest of the day at work to lose my feeling of oppression. I didn't tell Rose, but left her booking the acupuncture conference. Getting on with life was the best way to exorcise the unwelcome ghosts of Hashima. Being in Japan with Brett, seemed like a lifetime away, a different play with a different cast. Sometimes I panicked that I would forget.

11. A Gymnast's story.

I enjoyed the Acupuncture conference, although, just to spike my newly made plans to lighten up, I'd had to fore-go an exciting invitation to join Mark, Dominic, Pen and Angus at the opera, courtesy of Dom's corporate entertaining, in order to attend the conference. I was disappointed because having had a quiet time socially recently it seemed unfair that the invitation doubled up with the conference weekend. Mark and Dom were fun and I was enjoying their company. Dom was funny, charming and sparkling company. I was revising my first bad impression of him, he wasn't Mr Sensitive, but he wasn't an awful pushy idiot as I'd first thought. He worked hard and played hard too, but he was clever and interesting and the work his investment group did with the fortune they had made was mainly with young start up entrepreneurs. I got the impression he was more philanthropic than he wanted to let on. Mark was very different, quieter and harder to read, sometimes very endearing and I felt like we got on well, other times he seemed abstracted and distant. I wasn't quite sure where I stood with him.

I put my conference learning to good use almost immediately, to help a young gymnast. Luke was a pleasant dark- haired lad with dark eyes and eyelashes to die for. Only medium height, he looked powerfully built yet lithe. His mother a short dynamic lady with the same dark eyes, asked to come in to the assessment with him and after I'd checked Luke had no objections, we all went into the treatment room.

"Hi Luke, what brings you along today?"

"I've got this horrible, backache that keeps coming back" he said pointing to an area just below his ribs in the left- hand side. I've had an x-ray and a scan which don't show anything wrong so why am I in pain?"

I felt a flick of frustration, of all the health professionals he'd seen, no-one had explained that having pain does not always equal having visible damage. If nothing else, I wanted Luke to go away from Touch, understanding his pain may come from dysfunction not damage and how it could have occurred.

"Does it spread anywhere else?"

He shook his head

"Any symptoms going into your legs or funny sensations like pins and needles or numbness?"

"No, it is always in the same place."

"When do you get it?"

"Mainly after my training and it seems worst when I'm working on my ground work exercises - it absolutely kills me when I'm doing back flips. Problem is I have quite a few in my routine for the competition."

I empathised with the note of desperation in his voice. It can seem that elite sportsmen and women, gymnasts and performers have perfectly honed bodies, strong, supple, balanced. They achieve spectacular feats of performance, but often they do it in spite of muscle imbalances, areas of stiffness or weakness that you wouldn't suspect. To create the physical performance that they do and the illusion of symmetry, they borrow strength, support or trick mobility from elsewhere in the body to compensate for their weaknesses. If the trick movement is repeated often during training, the compensation itself causes pain and over time can lead to injuries or tissue damage. These faulty movement patterns or technique flaws, have a nasty habit of showing up at the most heart-breaking moments; just before a performance or a major competition, because training has been intensified.

Luke's back problem was a perfect example of this; he was training for the British championships. Doing well, could mean a place in the National squad, so he was training very hard. I needed Luke and his Mum to feel confident and trust me, so that I could help them get through this difficult time.

At this stage I didn't know the outcome, so my approach and explanations would be very important to build that trust. Mark and I had discussed communication skills last week, related to a training article he'd been asked to write. I made a mental note to tell Mark I'd been using some of his body language tips when I saw him.

Luke's Club Physio had treated the local, painful area in his back quite extensively, which settled the pain temporarily, only to see it return each time he returned to training. It seemed pointless to simply repeat what she had already done, so I chose a different tack and explained... "Sometimes, if treating the part of the body where you feel the pain isn't working, we have to ask why that area is getting overloaded and what else could be driving the symptoms."

"But I don't have pain anywhere else."

I nodded my understanding "Even if you don't, there may be bits of you that are stiff, weak or hyper-mobile that are affecting the way you move your back and causing it to become painful. Let's take a look shall we?"

He peeled off his tracksuit and trainers then stood up waiting for instructions, as the inevitable faint aroma of teenage trainers, many times worn, many times wet and dry, pervaded the room.

"OK, Luke, stand with your back to me, feet hip width apart, I'm going to look at your posture overall to start with."

As I stood back to observe, I noticed that Luke stood with an exaggerated inward curve in his low back, slightly rounded shoulders and his chin poked forwards. His muscular development was heavy across the shoulders giving the impression that he had a coat hanger under his skin. His upper abdominals were very defined but over-tight, pulling the lower ribs down and in and rounding his middle back. I suspected that this muscle imbalance made it hard for him to stabilise his low back correctly, because the deep transverse abdominals would be inhibited by their over enthusiastic namesakes. Importantly for him, I imagined those over tight upper abdominals would also make it difficult to expand the lower ribs and use the diaphragm correctly to breathe efficiently.

"Luke can you take a deep breath in please?"

As I suspected, his upper chest inflated massively, but there was very little lower rib or diaphragm movement. I got Luke to watch himself breath in the mirror and explained, "To get air into the lungs to provide oxygen for activity, the ribs must lift up and out to the horizontal from their resting position." I showed him on me, smoothing my tee shirt over my ribs so he could see the movement. "See them lift?" He nodded, "As they lift the lungs, which are attached to the ribs internally, are stretched. This makes the air pressure inside them fall and air flows in. The lower ribs are much longer than the upper ones, so when they lift up, they expand the lungs far more than the tiny upper ribs. The upper ribs should only be used as spare capacity for extreme situations. Because your upper abs are too tight and are binding the lower ribs down, you aren't breathing efficiently.

"Wow that's not good" he said with a little frown

"It's a problem for you as a gymnast. The diaphragm (which is a large dome shaped muscle that separates the chest from the abdomen) should flatten down as you breath in too. It squashes the abdominal contents and stretches the lungs, vertically this time, causing air to flow in. That is why we should see a rise and fall of the abdomen during breathing as the diaphragm moves. Because of your tight abs that isn't happening either."

"So, I'm stuffed!" he said. In that moment, as he deflected the seriousness of my explanation with his joke, he reminded me of Brett, who liked to cut to the chase using humour. The familiar tug of missing Brett pulled at me fleetingly.

"I wouldn't put it quite like that," I laughed, "but I can teach you to make your breathing a lot more efficient. As you breathe better, you'll be able to use the core stabilising muscles more easily which will protect your back. The deep abs are being overwhelmed at the moment by those over-dominant upper abs. You'll feel less tension in your neck and shoulders too because you won't be straining to get enough breath in by only using the upper ribs."

"Cool." He said "Sounds good."

Breathing well is cool. In the early days after Brett died, I felt like I couldn't breathe most of the time, but a lot of that was caused by stress. When I was able to think straight, I used the techniques I was teaching Luke, to breathe well. Breathing deep and calm, tricked my body into believing I wasn't stressed and helped me to control my muscle tension. Breathing properly helped my mood as well. I thought Luke could really benefit from breathing well, not just physically, but because it could help him prepare mentally and control performance nerves in competition.

"Now, can you raise both arms overhead."

As I watched the movement, it became apparent that to get both arms above his head, Luke had to arch his lumbar spine early in the movement and more obviously on the left. This created a sharp hinge across the back instead of a normal smooth, harmonious curve. His dorsal spine, the part where the ribs attach, remained very stiff too, normally it should extend as the arms move overhead.

"Luke, can I get you to stand back to the wall and this time, don't let your back arch off the wall as your arms go up"

This turned out to be very revealing, in order to raise his arms, he either had to arch his back or let his shoulder blades pop out of position sideways. Luke was also struggling to keep a flat back on the wall, and had to bend his hips and move his feet forward (as if sitting on perch stool) to stay flat. I placed my hands on the side of his chest and as he repeated the movement, tried to guide the shoulder blades to keep them tucked in. It was a struggle, his powerful muscles tried to follow their usual pattern and without using trick movements, he had quite limited range of movement in his shoulders.

"I can already see two things that are making you overuse the part of your back that is hurting. Latissimus dorsi is a broad sheet of muscle stretching from the pelvis right up to the shoulder. It's a really important muscle that generates power for shoulder rotation and movement when your body weight is hanging. You are so tight in your Lat muscles, that when you need to reach up they can't pay out enough to get your arms overhead. So, you borrow movement from your back and shoulder blades instead. Your dorsal spine is stiff too which isn't helping, so the borrowed movement is mainly coming from the segment of spine where your pain is."

"I didn't realise I was so tight"

It's not just your shoulders either, the muscles at the front of your hips are tight too, they can't pay out enough either when your hip swings back and it's the same bit of spine being over-worked to help the hips extend - double trouble.

"So that's why the pain keeps coming back even though we've had the back treated," said his Mum.

"Yes, I think so, treating the back is treating the symptom not the cause. So, I think we have we have our list of tasks to tackle."

"Will I be OK in time for the British - it's in six weeks-time?"

"I can't promise, six weeks is the bare minimum for soft tissues to heal, but I hope so."

I would do my best to get him there, if he missed the Championships and a shot at the England squad, the emotional scars could be slower to heal. I knew plenty about that and feeling bereaved isn't always about someone dying, we mourn lost dreams too. I kept that to myself and carried on, "You'll pick this up quickly, because you are very body aware. We can help offload the back in the meantime with sports tape to help with pain during training. I'd avoid the most painful moves for a week though and concentrate on the rehab exercises I'm going to teach you if you can."

"Can you write to his coach?" Luke's Mum asked, "He's going to want to understand all this."

"Yes, of course, but probably better if we talked it through. Also, if you have any recent camcorder film of Luke, we could watch together, so you can see what's happening when you do your routines too."

"We probably have some from his last competition," she said "I'll look it out."

His parents would suffer almost as much as Luke whilst we worked against the clock to try to get him fit. Treatment needed to be intensive to be successful, so would take up quite a lot of theirs and my time. I'd need to do some out of clinic time with him at the gym in my spare time as well. Although I would enjoy doing it, I felt a twinge of regret that I wouldn't be as free over the next few weeks to enjoy my new-found social life with Mark and the others. If I charged Luke's parents for all of my time, it would be expensive for them too, but I didn't want money to be an issue, I'd have to give it thought.

Over the next four weeks Luke, his coach and I worked intensively together with manual techniques, acupuncture and exercise. As I used the new fascial release acupuncture techniques I had learned at the conference to help release Luke's tight hip and shoulder muscles.

"You just like sticking pins in people Ellie." Luke said as we began one treatment session.

I laughed, "you're right."

We worked on mats, with gym balls and wobble boards to challenge his new posture and improve his core control even in unstable conditions. I went to the gym, where we progressed Luke's core work into exercises on his apparatus.

Getting out of the treatment room into Luke's training environment was great. The atmosphere was dynamic and Luke got all the benefits of working with his usual friends. The smell of the gym hit me every time I walked in; hot bodies, chalk and menthol embrocation, they combine to make a powerful elixir, probably on its own capable of enhancing performance.

Luke's Father took film of his training sessions each week and we saw the improvements from the treatment room and better control from the rehab. exercises, translate to more efficient technique in the gym. Compliant and so disciplined about doing what was needed to achieve his goals, Luke was a great patient. I would never have wished an injury on Luke, but had to confess I relished the challenge of working with him. I began to feel cautiously optimistic about the competition. It would be so good to see him overcome this huge setback and come back fighting.

We were going into the final two weeks before the competition when Mark dropped by the cottage. It was good to see him but I wondered what mood he'd be in. He found me with Luke's training schedules spread over my desk. As the practice had been busy, I decided to do some planning at home and was working on the last elements I wanted to achieve in terms of Physio treatment for Luke.

"Hey stranger, how are you doing?" Cheerful mood clearly, I thought.

"Hi Mark, I'm fine, come in. Do you fancy a coffee? Or there's a cold beer in the fridge."

"Coffee's fine," he said "I've hardly seen you the last few weeks, what've you been up to?"

He followed me into the kitchen and I explained "I've been treating a young guy and I've needed to do some sessions with him and his coach at training which has taken up quite a few evenings, on top of the usual evenings in the Clinic and a couple of Saturdays too. That's what I was doing when you arrived, sorting out his treatment plan for the last two weeks before his big competition."

"You work so hard Ellie, don't these talented youngsters have Physio's at their clubs? I thought all that stuff would be funded for them."

I handed him his coffee, "Don't get me started, the funding is appalling unless you've made the big time. Most of their care gets funded by their parents. This chap has a Club Physio - she does a few hours a week and is a bit run off her feet. She asked me to help out because his case was complicated and I'm more specialised than she is because of the training I did in Australia."

"That's a nice feather in your cap."

"It was lovely to be asked and it has been really interesting. I'm just fed up that there is no funding for him. So, I've thought about it and I might offer a sort of treatment bursary, so that he can get the treatment he needs at Touch. I've got to be careful though, he could need a lot of treatment and clearly sometimes it will be urgent, I can't afford to neglect my paying clients.

"I can see the dilemma, if you go broke, the clinic won't be there for anyone. And you've got to keep your own work/life balance right too Ellie, nobody's seen you for the last few weeks, you'll get burnout."

"Don't you nag me too, I've had Pen on the phone complaining she never sees me at the moment. It's impossible to please everyone and Luke does need help so he’s been my priority. Especially while he is still growing and maturing, it is so important that the youngsters are monitored properly."

"He’s a lucky lad, can I have a bursary to be pampered by you?”

"I'm not sure he would say I pamper him, he is normally begging for mercy!"

"I could cope with that too!”

I shot him a look.

“Joke, joke, don’t eat me. But seriously, that's a generous offer, it's one of the perks of running your own clinic I guess, you can choose to do something like that.”

"Well, I asked the boss and she said 'Yes'. It's a drop in the ocean in solving the overall funding problem, but from small acorns..."

He nodded, "That’s what I was hoping, if I begged for mercy, we might be able to start our own oak tree." Then before I had a chance to react to his flirting or even be quite sure he was flirting, he said, “Before you take it all on yourself, if funding his treatment will be a stretch for you, why don’t you think about asking someone else to help with the costs?"

“Like who?”

“Well Dom might consider it for one, he could afford to and might like to do something like that.”

“Do you think he would?”

"Look, I’ll ask him and then you two could talk about it if he’s interested.”

“That would be great Mark, thank you.”

“Changing the subject, I actually popped in to see if you fancied a game of tennis at the weekend? Dom's down and said he fancied a game, Pen's up for it as well."

Mark never ceased to amaze me, he was a curious mix of sensitive, kind, pragmatic, fun, moody, there was never a dull moment. He intrigued me. I realised he was waiting for an answer about the tennis, with a slightly amused look on his face. I flushed, having been caught wool gathering...

"Sounds good," I said "Sunday is best for me, let me know what time."

“Thought you’d drifted off there for a moment.” He swallowed the last of his coffee, "I’ll phone with the time tomorrow. I'll let you get on, I need to go and eat. But Ellie, you do work too hard, you look shattered." He gave me a soft kiss on the cheek and left me touching my cheek where he’d kissed me, alone with my planning. As he’d leaned in to me, I noticed that Mark smelt good, all Christian Dior and really yummy. It made a nice change from sweaty trainers, but I had no business thinking about how good Mark smelt, he was just a friend and I was in danger of crossing a boundary.

For a moment after he left, his warm energy still seemed to be in the room. I wasn't sure about the oak tree remark, for a moment I thought he was he flirting with me, but he moved on so quickly I wasn't sure. I smiled as I watched his car pull off the drive, would I mind if he was flirting? “I don’t know.” I answered myself crossly, “He’s a really good friend, don’t go there and blow it Ellie.”

Getting to know him had made a big difference to me, I didn’t want to lose him as a friend, and if we started a relationship and it all went wrong, I’d lose Dom as well. It may make things awkward with Pen and Angus too. ‘Friends’ was best, I decided.

I was genuinely looking forward to the tennis game on Sunday. I wasn’t going through the motions of accepting a social invitation like a robot, which I'd been doing since Brett died. Forcing myself to do social things, not actively looking forward to them, and for so long the idea of actually enjoying myself seemed wrong. I felt a frisson of remorse like a chilly breeze ruffling the leaves of a tree, but knew I had to put it aside. Having fun with Mark and Dom, made me see that picking up my life again was a good thing, it wasn't a betrayal. Brett was no longer here and I had to live with the living, he would never have wanted my lifc to be only a memorial to his.

I looked back to my papers on the desk - Luke, at just seventeen, was also a lesson in resilience if I needed further encouragement.

The next day I saw Luke in the clinic for his last 'hands on' treatment and popped in to the gym after work to watch him run through his mat routine. He looked good. I had a chat with his coach and we both thought he was ready to compete.

12. Anyone for tennis?

Sunday dawned bright and clear. I got up early to walk the dogs before getting ready to play tennis. I'd played at school and with a club when I lived in France, but it was ages since I'd touched a racquet and I rather hoped the others weren't too brilliant either. I was sure Pen didn't play much, because she'd never mentioned it. We'd see if the boys were secret Aces...

In a nutshell, they weren't. Mark, like me, had played at school and the odd social games. Dom had played more squash and with his unorthodox, transferred technique, managed some fiendish mis-hits with odd spin.

"Oh no!" I yelled as the ball stopped dead and then veered off sharply sideways, "that is so unfair after I've sprinted up from the base-line. I thought I had that."

Dom winked at me, "All meticulously planned."

"Dominic Lancaster you are such a liar, that was a fluky squash shot if ever I saw one!"

"Mark, keep your partner under control, she's casting aspersions on my partner's playing skills," Pen called, "very unsporting!"

"Quite right too," Mark replied "he is so jammy." Then to me he said quietly, "Serve to his backhand he isn't as strong there, we'll pick up points."

I was surprised, although we were playing for fun, I sensed Mark wanted to win. I got a glimpse of a competitive streak I'd never seen before. I liked it, it made me feel he wasn't a push-over for all his gentle kindness.

"I'll just ace him down the line." I joked, then wished I hadn't, as I promptly served up a double fault.

In the end, our hour was up before the game was decided and we adjourned to the Prince of Wales, a small whitewashed stone pub that smelt of log fires and old wood. Angus joined us for a lazy lunch and a thorough debrief of the Game. Eventually the talk around the table turned to current affairs and Dom was talking about Lloyds - more precisely the Lloyds Names and what a disastrous time they were having at the moment.

"Some of them stand to lose their skin," said Dom.

"Surely most of them will have millions stashed in other places," said Angus.

"Not necessarily," Dom replied "they have very heavy liabilities and the asbestosis scandals in America are building momentum, nobody knows yet what their full liabilities are or how many claims there will be."

I felt a small pinprick of anxiety as I listened to them chatting, part of the loan for my practice had come from my Godfather, James McLeod. I knew he could be affected, because Mum reverently said "He's a Lloyds name you know..." to me nearly every time she and Dad went out with Uncle James. I wondered how he was faring. I wondered too if it could put in question the loan he'd made me. I had only last week seen interest rates hiking yet again, which immediately added to my loan repayment bill, and had been thankful that not all my business loan was with the bank. It would make things very tight at Touch if I had to extend my bank loan. I sometimes worried that I wasn't cut out to be a business woman, finances prayed on my mind. I'd speak to James when I got home, forewarned is forearmed. I felt my upper body sag, 'Please let it all work out.' I half thought, half prayed.

"You OK Ellie?" Mark asked turning away from the group, "you've gone a bit quiet."

"Yes, of course, just Dom talking about the problems at Lloyds, some of my loan is from a family friend who could be caught up in this."

"Do you think he might withdraw the loan?"

"I really don't know."

Just talking about it made my stomach do somersaults, I had hated doing all the loan negotiating, I felt more comfortable in the treatment room than in a bank. I was so relieved once the loans were set up and I'd assumed that was that, unless I defaulted on payment. At least I had a business track record now, so hopefully the bank would extend my loan, especially as most of it was for the actual bricks and mortar.

Mark broke in on my galloping thoughts, "Hopefully, it won't come to that. I'm lucky haven't got a loan."

I didn't reply, it was OK for him, his business just needed him and a briefcase. Mine needed space and expensive equipment.

"You know there are other investors that will put finance into a good company too..." he continued.

"Vaguely, well not really," I said, "hopefully I'm worrying about nothing. Anyway, it's not your problem."

"Ellie...". He tried to say something else but was interrupted...

"Anyone for another drink?" Dom asked.

All the guys agreed to another beer before they left and they turned to me...

"Not for me, I need to head for home and give the dogs another run." I wasn't sure why I had blurted all that out about my loans. Part of me hoped Mark didn't think I was being neurotic and part of me felt cross, he didn't seem that concerned.

"Mine need a stretch too," said Pen "shall we run them together? We could walk along the river for a change. You OK to walk back if I head home now Angus?"

"Sure, the three of us can walk up across the fields together."

I got up to kiss the lads goodbye and said "I think I'm going to be stiff tomorrow, I can feel my legs tightening up already - out of practice clearly."

"I'll send Mark over to give you a massage," said Dom as I leant over to kiss him.

I felt a blush creep up my face, bloody Dom!

"Anytime," said Mark looking as embarrassed as I felt.

"Guys!" I said laughing to cover my embarrassment, "cancel that last round, I think you've had quite enough beer."

13. Questions with no answers.

As I sat in the car, I thought briefly about that massage with Mark, and smiled to myself, "Could be nice," I decided, then remembered I was actually cross with him. Dom was probably just joking about anyway, but I realised it was the second time that week I had wondered where my friendship with Mark was leading.

I arrived first at the river. As I waited for Pen, the dogs snuffled about and I looked at the quiet estuary picture in front of me. Flood defence walls snaked a circular path around the water meadows, with deep dykes populated by coots, swans and ducks that glided amongst the deep reed beds. The forked river, tide in today, glittered blue in the sun. When I first came to Essex, I found the scenery flat, but as I looked now and noticed the boats in the marina, their halyards clanging like distant cow bells and the subtle shading of foliage from the ash-blonde reed heads with their silver green leaves to straw coloured grasses and dark green shrubs, I acknowledged this palette had its own discreet beauty. The tidal estuary gave off a smell of salt water and the sea beyond, which tingled in my nose - quite different from the green smell of a freshwater river.

Pen's car drew up and two piebald flashes swept past me as her Pointers rushed to join my two dogs, their greeting rituals of play bows and bouncing invitations to the chase, the unspoken language of established friendship.

As she caught up with her dogs and we set off, Pen said, "I enjoyed that, it was fun playing tennis again. Good to have a group to go out with now too, Angus really likes having Mark and Dom about, he misses all the banter you get working in a company now he's on the farm."

"I forgot he used to work in London."

"I don't think he really wants to be back there, but I worry about him getting lonely, so I'm glad the lads have moved next door. Mark's nice, and I think he's a bit sweet on you."

"Not you as well! What's the matter with everyone? We're just good friends." I didn't want Pen to think there was anything in it, in case we were both wrong. "You're imagining things!" I gave her a friendly push and laughed.

"Well as I keep saying, you've got to take the plunge sometime and you and Mark would make a great couple."

"Come on, lets walk, we aren't a couple."

I didn't have a chance to dwell on the idea of Mark as a boyfriend for long, my call to James McLeod when I got home preoccupied me.

"Hi Uncle James, how are you?"

"Ellie how good to hear from you, how's the Clinic going?"

"Well, touch wood! I'm busy most of the time and working extra hours."

"That's great Ellie, your Dad has told me how hard you're working."

I wasn't sure how to get to the point and ended up blurting out, "Uncle James, you would tell me if the loan you gave me wasn't convenient, anymore wouldn't you?"

"My dear girl of course I would, whatever makes you ask?"

"It's just I've seen all the reports about the trouble within Lloyds and I know that you could be affected."

"The value of your investment can go down as well as up? It's worrying, I won't deny it and I expect to lose some money, all of us do, but there isn't any immediate concern. Bless you for asking. You don't need to worry, about me."

He turned the conversation firmly back to social bits and pieces and I had to leave it at that. But there was enough constraint in his voice for me to feel not entirely convinced.

As I put the phone down, I glanced out of the window, the garden looked inviting. I walked out to sit in my favourite spot, the curved trunk of a graceful willow tree that fitted my form perfectly. The gnawing anxiety that had started in the Pub, crescendo-ed into a moment of panic and I felt a bit sick. Poor Uncle James, how awful for him and a massive blow for me if I had to re-finance. How terrible for the claimants in America too, they had clearly been unfairly treated.

I had always felt the success or failure of Touch would be in my own hands, but it seemed that the ripples of something that happened so far away, may come to intrude uninvited. Thoughts and half conceived plans jostled in my head, but I finally succumbed to the calm of the evening garden, and realised there was no point in worrying tonight. Maybe if it came to it, I could ask Mark for some professional help, he helped companies all the time.

It had been a beautiful day with a bright blue sky. As I watched the sun dip below the horizon and dusk began to settle, the blue remained, but appeared clouded behind a fine sooty veil as night extinguished the bright day. Eventually only stars twinkled like hope in the darkness.

Despite my praiseworthy intention not to worry, I slept fitfully with jumbled dreams and Monday morning found me feeling ragged. I had a busy list at the clinic which spread right through the day with only a short break for lunch and time to clear some admin. About six o'clock, as I was writing letters, Rose poked her head round the office door and said "Can you spare a minute, Luke's here."

I walked through into reception and said "Hi Luke come on into the office."

I could see immediately something was wrong. Luke's face as he hobbled towards me, said it all. He looked drawn and deflated.

"What on earth has happened?"

"Ellie, I've broken my toe."

"How?"

"It was stupid, I caught it between two mats at training, sort of stubbed it. But it really hurt straight away. Mum took me to A and E and the x-ray shows the fourth toe is broken."

"Oh no! Luke I'm so sorry." Sorry, I was devastated by the unfairness of it all, so goodness knows how he felt. His outward manner was stoic but his beautiful brown eyes clouded with despair, held a mute appeal, a glimmer of half a hope that I might have a rabbit to pull out of the hat that would let him compete. I did not. No amount of Physio was going to make a fracture right in three or four days.

After all his hard work, Luke was not destined to get to the Championships that year. Elite athletes have to be made of tough stuff and injury is a nemesis which haunts them. Having the fortitude to cope with this kind of set-back is part of competitive sport. I thought that after the frustration and disappointment passed, Luke would find that mental toughness. He was disciplined, he did not give up, I'd seen that. I felt he would wait for the toe to heal and refocus his goals to the following year. I hoped he would compete successfully, time would tell.

To ease the bitter pill, I spoke to him about the treatment bursary. Over the weekend, Dom had offered a very generous sum that would easily cover Physiotherapy expenses, with some left over for kit and travel. It was far more than I could have afforded. When I tried to thank Dom, he'd just said it was good business and that he'd ask Luke to do some publicity with him for the company magazine and to wear the company logo on any training kit.

It seemed I was right in my suspicions, there was more to Dom than his 'Jack the Lad' exterior after all.

Luke was red faced and incoherent with surprise, but thrilled I'm sure. I gave him Dominic's contact details so that he and his parents could get in touch and said that I'd see him in about three weeks-time to get him back into training. I hoped he left feeling a bit more positive.

I remained in an odd mood, delighted with Dom's bursary for Luke, devastated about the championships and really low about the possibility of the business being in trouble.

Luke and I had a few things in common it seemed, despite all my hard work, life sometimes wasn't fair and I may be needing some mental toughness and regrouping of my own, if Touch wasn't to become a victim of the financial crisis. Feeling rather sorry for myself, I decided without much success, that I needed to take a leaf out of his book and toughen up.

14 Pam's story.

Summer began to drift lazily into Autumn - the days were noticeably shorter and in just a month the clocks would change and my leisurely evening walks after work, in the cool of the day would be curtailed. Because I worked inside, I needed to get out into the fresh air to clear my head and am an unashamed tree hugger, or perhaps more of a tree leaner. For me there is no finer place to regain perspective than leaning against a tree, imagining my feet sending roots deep into the ground, the trunk behind to steady me. As soon as I feel grounded again, I look up through the canopy, reaching up with my arms like branches and let go of all my worries into the ether. Then my mind runs free, thoughts and ideas scudding across my brain like the clouds above me. Often unbidden, comes a solution to the problem or the bright idea I seek.

I called the tree in my garden Grandmother Willow after the Pocahontas story. Her rustling leaves whisper gently and that me-shaped dent in her trunk, is perfect for sitting or leaning. I have broken my heart and grieved for Brett there, in solitude, sobbing great gobs of pain from the centre of my being, often left gasping, spent, lungs heaving. Listening without judgement, Grandmother Willow always seems to comfort me with her whisperings of hope and recovery. She knows about recovery, one day, about three years ago in the great storm, I watched aghast as she was hit by lightning and struck asunder, cleaved as if by a mighty sword, burned out by an avenging flame. I thought my beautiful tree was dead. But, little by little, in the Spring, new shoots grew from her base and they are rapidly becoming strong branches again - I take hope from her resilience when my resolve falters.

Looking at my Clinic list for the following day, Tuesday, I was surprised to see Pam Bane's name there. I knew Pam fairly well, she had lived in the town for many years and was a well-known figure, heavily involved with local fund-raising and with many local organisations including the church. When I first set up the clinic, she came in to the rooms on the opening day, to welcome me and wish us well. She left with a promise of five homemade cakes for the Church fete and sponsorship for the "Splat the Rat" stall!

"Come to the fete, I'll introduce you to some people," she had said cheerfully as she left and good as her word, I left the fete knowing the Doctors receptionists, the local Pharmacist, the Postmistress and anyone else she could think of, who might spread the word about the Clinic.

When she arrived for her appointment and I showed her into the treatment room, she looked outwardly as I have always known her, a plump lady in her mid-fifties with a pink-cheeked, kind face, but on looking a little closer, I noticed she seemed slightly drawn and had blue shadows smudging the skin under her eyes.

"Hello Pam, it's lovely to see you, but I'm sorry you've got a problem, what brings you here today?"

"Well, it's not exactly Physio," she said fidgeting on her chair, "You do all the relaxation bits don't you? I've got something coming up that I'm dreading. Being silly really, I'm sure it will be fine, but I thought this might help."

"It's a very good idea Pam." I waited for her to go on and in the lengthening silence I wondered what had happened.

Under her brisk and cheerful manner, Pam noticed a lot about people and quietly supported many in our community who needed help; a lift to the supermarket here, a pop-in visit there, or company on trips to the hospital - which was twelve miles away and tricky to get to without a car.

She continued, "I had a mammogram about a fortnight ago, completely forgot all about it straight after. But I've had a call from the Doctor, something doesn't look right and I have to go for an appointment and a biopsy on Friday. I have taken so many people to these appointments and I always say reassuring things, but now it's my turn, I'm really scared. I'm sorry to be such a nuisance."

Pam was one of the first people apart from Pen that I'd told about Brett. It happened when I did some free 'taster' relaxation sessions at a pamper day for carers that she organised. Packing away at the end of the day, she'd invited me to Wisteria Cottage, her beautiful home for a cuppa. Placing a steaming mug of nut-brown tea and a wedge of moist fruit cake in front of me she'd said, "I worry about you, Ellie."

"Oh dear, why?"

"You seem very cheerful and always busy with your dogs and helping other people, but your eyes are sad sometimes...tell me to mind my own business if I am speaking out of turn."

And just like that, I'd found myself explaining about Brett. I knew what I said would go no further, Pam was many things, but I had never heard her gossip about anyone.

She'd listened then said, "That's a tough break my girl and all you can do is keep on living, which you don't need me to tell you. I'm always here if you need someone to talk to."

I'd mentally blessed her for being so concerned, but not overwhelming me with advice.

Over the years we had remained friends and I let her bully me into doing all sorts of community events, but she had never been a patient before.

Hearing her confession about being frightened, I realised, this stoic lady must be terrified or she wouldn't be here at all. "You're not a nuisance Pam, much better to be honest about how you're feeling."

"The thing is, I've got an awful feeling about this and I feel panicky every time I think about it. Just being stupid."

Pam was being so hard on herself, "You're allowed to feel frightened when something like this happens." So many people who spend their lives helping others, don't like asking for help themselves. "You of all people understand how important it is to have support Pam. Managing problems is often about knowing who and when to ask for help, so you did right to come."

Peter, Pam's husband was a retired investment banker. Although retired, he continued to be involved with several charities and an arts foundation. What I'd describe as a proper grown up! He always seemed a little aloof to me though, and I got the impression that he only tolerated the parochial events which Pam was involved in. I'd seen him smile in a fond way at all her bustling and activity as one does at a kitten's engaging tricks. Her use of the word "obliged" rather shocked me, it seemed wrong that she felt unable to bother her husband with such trivia as the possibility of breast cancer.

"I'm free on Friday, I only had office work planned, no clinic, so I can come with you to the hospital if you like. I need to pick up a couple of journal articles from the medical library there. I have a lecture coming up, so I can do that whilst we're there."

"I can't possibly ask you to do that!" she said, I had clearly taken her by surprise.

"Why ever not, it's no problem, I'm sure you'd do the same for me - what time is your appointment?"

"Well if you're sure you don't mind...it's at eleven o'clock and I would be very grateful."

"I'll pick you up around ten. But in the meantime, lets teach you some relaxation today, whilst you're here. Pop up on the couch comfortably and I'll run through a simple technique you can practice."

There are a number of different relaxation methods to choose from and people respond differently to each one. I decided to use relaxation visualisation for Pam, as time was short before her appointment and I could back up today's session with some visualisations to play at home that I'd written and recorded. She could take the cassette with her to the Hospital and play it on a Walkman, to help with nerves.

I settled Pam on her back with soft pillows under her head and a roll under her knees to allow her back to settle comfortably on the couch. I covered her with a light blanket and dimmed the overhead lights slightly. Once she was settled, I put on a quiet instrumental track and sat at the bottom of the bed.

"Where is your favourite place Pam? Beach, woodlands, on a boat..."

"I love walking through woods in the Autumn."

"OK, we'll use that as a theme, lets concentrate on your breathing to start - let the air flow in through your nose and easily down into your chest, easy in and easy out. No need to breathe deeply, just easy breaths in and out. As you breathe out, let your body relax into the couch, heavy and relaxed, comfortable and safe. This is your time to take a journey in your imagination, guided by my voice..."

I gently walked her, in her imagination, through my favourite woods. As I remembered every detail of my walks there in the Autumn describing the colours of the leaves and the way the light slanted through the trees, I wove a story, invoking the smells and sounds of the wood, painting a word picture for her to become immersed in, in order to relax. Then slowly, after about ten minutes, brought her attention back to her breathing and back into the room around her at the end of the session.

As Pam left behind the scene I'd created for her, she yawned and stretched out, that was amazing Ellie, it was just like being there. I love trees. I suppose you want me to sit up now I'm not sure I can move, I drifted off so far.

"Just sit up slowly, make sure you don't feel light headed - the relaxation can just lower your blood pressure a little temporarily."

"No, I feel fine," she replied, "actually I think I could nod off.

"Well, have a glass of water before you leave, make sure you feel alright to drive and why don't you treat yourself to a snooze when you get home?"

"Might well do that," she replied, "thanks Ellie."

"My pleasure – Pam, take this cassette, it has a very similar visualisation on it called The Autumn Lake, use it to take time out every day and properly relax. Then you could bring it in with you on Friday or use it when you feel nervous. It's important to use it regularly though, it's much easier to relax if you've practised. The body knows what to do, because the technique feels familiar - like an old friend and your brain just responds to the cues even if you're feeling stressed or nervous."

The Friday of the appointment dawned as a crisp, misty Autumn day rather like Pam's visualisation. I drove to Wisteria Cottage, her pretty thatched, pargetted Cottage on the edge of the village, as agreed at about a quarter to ten. I knocked on the front door and heard Pam's footsteps as she approached the door and opened it. She was wearing a smart suit that pulled slightly across the hips. The jacket was open, mainly I suspect because the buttons strained if it was closed. It was a little old fashioned and I was surprised to see her dressed like that. I was more used to seeing her either in cords with a blouse and V-necked jumper or a tweed skirt and twin set.

"I can't think why I'm all dressed up," she said ruefully, "the Consultant won't be interested in what I'm wearing, he'll be seeing what's wrong with me, but somehow it makes me feel more confident and I need that today! Trouble is I've been eating too many cakes and scones and I've expanded widthways. Suit's a bit tight - never mind."

What she usually wore suited her life much better than what she had on today, but I said she looked lovely - this was not a day for the unvarnished truth. Her eyes strayed from the hall mirror to the green tweed coat hanging from a peg on the hall coat stand. Her wellies were underneath and an assortment of hats, scarves and gloves tangled affectionately on the shelf behind the door.

"I would prefer to be out walking on a sunny morning like this and I have cakes to make for the church sale."

"I'm sure Pam, it's a pain, but it needs to be done."

Pam looked back at her reflection in the hall mirror for a moment and straightened her skirt, "well now! No point in dithering... The quicker you go, the quicker you know!" Then flicked me an unconvincing smile.

I touched her lightly on the shoulder in solidarity - there really were no words.

The breast unit was exemplary, and the process ran on oiled wheels. A nurse consultation first, with explanations about the biopsy and some leaflets to read about the department. Bloods were taken for testing. Then the Consultant chat, the less pleasant biopsy and the start of the anxious wait. Finally, back with the Nurse, reassurance that many biopsies turned out to be negative and we were back outside heading for the car.

"You alright?" I asked.

"Bit shell shocked and a bit sore but alright I think. The next ten days will seem like an eternity."

We chatted about this and that on the way home, a reflex, to introduce some normality into the all-encompassing nightmare.

"Let me know how you get on," I said as I dropped her back home.

Pam's results came back positive. She rang me to say that she had been back to the breast unit and had an appointment to go back to the hospital. The Consultant felt that she was going to need a mastectomy. Peter was home by then, so Pam declined my offer of a lift as he would take her. I was sad for her, she had been so afraid and it was almost as if she had a presentiment of what was going to happen. I remembered the awful presentiment I'd had on Hashima about losing Brett and hoped this was not going to be the same. Pam said she was coping and the Hospital were being very supportive. She couldn't believe how quickly she was having the operation.

I phoned after the surgery, when she was back at home and popped in to visit.

"How are you?" I asked as I settled into the large padded armchair and Peter brought us both a cup of tea.

"A bit uncomfortable," she said "but better now the drain is out."

"Not overdoing it?" I asked.

"No, no, I'm taking it very steady and doing my exercises every two hours," she said lifting her arm as proof.

"Oh well done."

"I'm just waiting for my test results, they took away some lymph nodes as well and did a body scan, but I feel fine in myself."

Talk drifted to other things and I left trying to feel hopeful that Pam was on the road to recovery, but with a horrible doubt that I kept pushing down, because of what had happened to Brett I knew the worst could happen. One thing was for certain life could never be taken for granted, Pam was an institution, and yet here she was so vulnerable, it was horrible to see. I needed to get on with my own life, not keep putting it off, none of us know when time will run out.

15. Invitation to murder.

Mark phoned out of the blue at the beginning of November. "Hi Ellie, I wondered what you're doing on the 25th, it's a Saturday. I've got a 'plus one' invitation from an old schoolfriend to his evening wedding reception up in London, somewhere along the Embankment. Dom will be going too. I thought it looked fun, they're having a swing band, so good excuse to get glam-ed up."

"Oh goodness, I haven't been to a posh frock do for ages." I hesitated wondering why he'd asked me, surely one of his old friends would fit in better or why not one of Dom's wonder girls? One of his dating agency women, I thought huffily, then remembered my promise to live life a little and lighten up.

Flushing with embarrassment about my nasty thoughts and glad he was on the phone, not here, I said "Thank you for thinking of me, just let me check," I pretended to look in my diary knowing full well the page would be empty, "Let me see..." I faked nonchalance, "No, that's all good, nothing on that night, I'd love to come." That had torn it, now I'd have to go. Oh God, was this a date? Or more likely, I was just his last resort, I thought crossly.

"Brilliant Ellie, I'll look forward to it, seems like ages since we met up."

It had been a couple of weeks since we'd met; the last time was for a popcorn and movie night at Angus and Pen's and we'd laughed ourselves silly over some stupid horror movie. That was the good thing about Mark, when he was on form, he was easy to be with. It was just that we seemed to take two steps forward, one step back and I didn't know where I stood with him. I wasn't sure if I fancied him, if he fancied me. Sometimes we were friends, other times I thought he was flirting. It was all a bit complicated. Neither of us had a partner at the moment, so it was good to have someone to go out with. 'Think of him as someone to practice your skills on' I thought and see what happens...

He cut in across my random thoughts, "I thought we could drive in."

"Good idea, if you drive in, I'm happy to drive home. I never drink much anyway, so it's no hardship."

"I may take you up on that."

As I put down the phone, I realised that I did feel quite excited, November is always a bit dreary and the wedding would be something to look forward to. I had nothing to wear of course and my mind raced forward, planning a shopping expedition to find something suitable to wear, when I remembered my red dress. It was a vintage 1940's New Look style in flame-red silk taffeta, that set my hair and pale skin off. I'd only worn it once, back in Australia and I wasn't sure how I'd feel about wearing it again, the night I'd worn it, turned out to be my first date with Brett...

Max, Annie, Brett and I had been invited to a murder mystery evening set in Casablanca. Brett's character was the American Playboy Night Club owner, I was a young

American woman with a dark past. Of course, a Casablanca theme was just the excuse Brett needed to don a white tux and pretend to be Humphrey Bogart! Not to be outdone, I secretly went off to a vintage clothes shop and found my amazing dress. Nipped in waist and full skirt, to just above the ankle, over lots of stiff petticoats. The boned bodice sat off my shoulders with a deep fold down and I felt a million dollars in it. Eat your heart out Ingrid Bergman! I kept it a secret from everyone until the night of the Murder mystery.

Dressed as a mysterious (supposedly Austrian) Countess in a slinky figure-hugging gown and wrap, Annie was sophisticated and gorgeous, with Max somewhat less romantically attired as a French resistance fighter in a collarless shirt and beret. When I walked into the sitting room of the flat with my hair curled and styled like Rita Hayworth, Brett's jaw dropped slightly, "Wow you look beautiful Ellie, *here's looking at you kid*," he made a mock bow and extended his crooked arm, on which I rested my gloved hand. We set off for the Murder Mystery in merry mood.

I was the murderess it turned out, unmasked at the end of the game only by Annie with her sharp brain and uncanny knack of asking the right questions. She was ably assisted by my complete inability to lie without a tell-tale blush giving me away. As we left, and were all, with the exception of Max, looking so suave, Brett suggested we go to the rooftop bar at the Hilton for a nightcap. Annie and Max declined, he was on duty the next day, so Brett and I went alone.

I can't quite describe how beautiful Sydney is on a balmy, warm evening, redolent of night-scented flowers, back lit by stars and with the reflection of the city lights on the water. After our sophisticated and eye-wateringly expensive drink, viewing the city by night and listening to the cocktail piano, we elected to take one of the small ferries and then walk home rather than call a cab. As we walked, we laughed about the evening, chatted some Physio shop-talk - I was so happy. We walked under the Frangipani tree at the front of our building and I paused momentarily to enjoy its sweet perfume. Brett paused too and bent to kiss me, lightly brushing my lips. Surprised, I closed my eyes and briefly touched my fingers to my lips, then grazing my bottom lip with my teeth, I tasted the kiss. A glint of moonlight reflected, as his eyes held mine, an unasked question forming as he looked down. Seeing the answer, he wordlessly held out his hand and led me into the building. As the door of the flat closed, the stillness inside enveloped us, at odds with my ferociously beating heart. He stopped to kiss me again, featherlight and teasing.

"Yes?"

"Yes." I replied softly.

I felt like I was falling, falling into his dark eyes, which did not leave mine, but melted from darkly intense to gently smiling, as he led the way to his room. I felt liquid and lost to myself as he brushed my hair aside gently and trailed kisses lazily down the side of my neck and across my bare shoulder. More hungrily, he unzipped the red silk, pushing it aside. The dress slid away without resistance and folded into a puddle of red silk at my feet. I stepped out of its containment and into the freedom of my lover's arms without hesitation.

Powerful memories, hauntingly real, I sank onto the bed and closed my eyes, surely, he would be there again when I opened them?

He wasn't, just the stillness of my room. How stupid to torture myself! Brett was gone and as I unpacked the red dress from its protective cover, I wasn't sure I could bear to wear it again. But, I stepped into it anyway and looked at my reflection. To entomb such a beautiful dress forever in acid-free tissue would be a travesty. Made to be worn, admired and spun around life's dance-floor, the dress was coming out with me to the wedding reception!

On the day of the wedding reception, after the usual dog walk, I indulged myself in a pamper day. Some serious repair work was needed on my feet before they could be displayed in sandals. They had seen rather too much of the inside of wellies in the last six weeks! Pen came over in the afternoon to help me put big rollers in my hair and I got her to do the nails on my right hand. Rubbish with a nail varnish brush in my left hand, I knew I would make a rogue stroke every now and then that would splodge colour onto the skin. Then as soon as I tried to repair the damage with a cotton bud and remover, things would just go from bad to worse.

"Don't touch anything," ordered Pen when the second coat of varnish was in place without mishap. "I'll go and make some tea, you can drink yours through a straw. I was a nervous wreck trying to get that varnish on straight, don't you dare smudge your nails."

"This is why I never wear it usually, what a palaver. Still, if we're sitting with Dom and one of his wonder girls, I'd better not let the side down."

"You're going to look fab," she replied, which struck me as funny, as I caught sight of myself in the mirror with rollers in, a white face mask gradually setting to stone on my face and fingers splayed wide by balls of cotton wool, like some weird lizard.

"Don't laugh!" She said, disappearing to make tea, "you'll crack the mask."

Mark was picking me up at five thirty to be in London for seven. By five fifteen, I was dressed and ready with my hair tumbling in curls over one shoulder and a haze of Van Cleef and Arpels "First" giving me confidence. In the kitchen with their feet up on the half door, the dogs clearly wondered why they couldn't come in.

Just before fivc thirty, I heard Mark's car pull up, the 'thunk' of his door shutting, followed by a knock at my front door. I grabbed my clutch bag and a spangled wrap (kindly donated by Pen) and opened the door.

Mark looked at me and grinned, then looked expectantly over my shoulder. "I've come to pick up Ellie, is she ready?"

"Ha, Ha!"

"You look lovely - twirl!"

I did a twirl and struck a "ta-dah" pose.

"Yes, perfect!"

"Well thank you, kind Sir," I replied "you scrub up well yourself." Mark looked very handsome indeed, the dark dinner suit looked great on his tall, slender form and he wasn't wearing any hideous frills, just a plain dress shirt. He had also managed to tame his wavy hair and the effect made him seem altogether more sophisticated. I was impressed, and it occurred to me again that I could be persuaded to cross the 'being just friends' line. Who knew? The red dress may work its magic again.

"Shall we?" He said.

I followed him out to the car, smoothed my petticoats carefully as I sat in the passenger seat and we set off. Before we left, Mark showed me on his A-Z where the hotel was and had thoughtfully marked up the page before too.

"I know my way to the embankment, but I'll need you to give me directions from there."

"It seems an absolute rule, that wherever you are going, the roads you need are always right in the centre crease or niftily in a corner of any map book, so you need at least four pages to do about quarter of a mile." I looked with misgiving at the misaligned roads in the centre of the page. The one we needed to find, disappeared straight into the centre crease. "I will try not to launch us into the Thames!"

"Oh well, if we end up doing the magical mystery tour it's not the end of the world."

Prophetic words... However, it was not on my watch as navigator that anything happened!

The journey was good, Mark explained about the people who'd be there. A lot of them were old school friends and he made me laugh recounting some of the antics their crew got up to at school. Mark had been a day pupil at a Prep. School near Guildford, Dom a border, but it seemed Dom had spent a good deal of time with Mark and his family. "Dom's folks were based out in Africa, his Father was in the Diplomatic Corps," he explained, "so he didn't really have anyone here in the UK, except an Auntie who had him to stay for the short holidays. My Mum and Dad took him under their wing. We were good friends, so he came to us for exeats, and they included him in our picnic on sports day, those kinds of things."

I began to see where their closeness had grown from and also wondered whether Dom had always been an outgoing person, or whether his charm and extrovert personality had started as a survival tactic to mask the difficulties of a small boy away from home, on another continent.

With its great buildings illuminated; the Tower of London, Tower Bridge and St. Pauls, nothing beats a drive through the City at night. I gazed my fill, then concentrated on guiding us to the back of the hotel where the reception was, to leave the car. Safely parked, we walked to the hotel's main entrance.

Navigating an old, but beautifully polished revolving door, into the plush foyer, my heels clicked on the polished marble floor as we followed directions to the ballroom. It felt a bit intimidating to be walking into a room full of people who all knew each other, but I comforted myself that my dress looked great and I had a very handsome man on my arm. I felt confident Mark would look after me, grumpy he may be sometimes but he was never bad mannered. At first glance, the room seemed crowded with people and a hubbub of chatter and laughter swelled out like a tsunami as we opened the door. Ladies' dresses sparkled colour, like jewels cast randomly across black velvet. They off-set the tailored darkness of the men.

The bride, Sarah, radiant in white lace over silk with her long ash-blonde hair nestling heavily in a pearl studded snood, stood at the head of the receiving line with Tom her husband and their proud parents. We said all that was proper and Mark was hugged warmly all the way along, he was clearly a favourite.

"Phew," he said running a finger under his collar, "it's more crowded than I thought." He deftly swept two glasses of champagne off a passing tray, handed one to me and steered me through the crowd with a nod here and a touch on the shoulder there. Being tall, he had spotted Dom and our table group over the heads of the other guests. Just before we reached them, he turned and said "Thank you for coming Ellie, really, I mean it."

Before I had a chance to reply, Dom hailed us and the moment was gone. We were drawn into the gang and shortly after, called to our table.

Dom's partner for the evening, Vale was American and yet another beauty. She and I were the only non-wives around the table and the only newbies to the group, which threw us into alliance. She was very good company, quick witted and funny, she reminded me of Annie except she was so tall. I liked her a lot. Something in the way she and Dom exchanged glances made me wonder if this girl was destined to be more special than the others. I hoped she lasted, she was a whole lot less scary than most of his wonder women. I wondered how Claire had fitted in with the group, had she been good friends with the wives? They all seemed friendly and included me in the chat and I wondered what they were thinking about me and how I measured up to Claire. Mark had said she was beautiful inside and out, I certainly wasn't confident that described me. A couple of them were a bit nosey, almost like they were vetting me to see if I was suitable for their friend. I felt a bit defiant initially, but then realised I'd have been the same, if roles had been reversed, they didn't want him to get hurt.

After dinner, as the band launched into a Frank Sinatra medley Mark took my hand, "May I?"

"With pleasure." I'd loved dancing since I was seven. I'd rehearsed for my junior dance medals as a youngster, in the village hall and dreamed of a "Come Dancing" style puff ball dress, one of the ones my dance teacher made. Mum thought the dress my Nan altered from the jumble sale was very pretty and quite nice enough, so I never did glide over the floor in one of these much-coveted confections. Mum had little sympathy for fanciful yearnings!

Mark took me by surprise as he took me in hold, and lightly but firmly swept me off into a Foxtrot.

"You can dance properly! What a dark horse you are..."

"One of the few valuable skills that expensive school taught me."

We danced for a few numbers, then slightly out of breath, left thc dance floor to get a cold drink. A large, heavily built chap, with a very red face and a large paunch, which strained to burst out between the buttons of his dress shirt, half collided with Mark and stumbled drunkenly sideways before steadying himself. He began to say he was sorry, when he stopped, stared at us both and said "Mark Roxshhhhbury," in a beery slur. "Peter Parkshhon...Parky."

"Oh yes, hi Parky." Mark replied holding out his hand.

"Good to sheee you, and thish is Claire, different hair," he blundered on, scrutinising me owlishly with his bloodshot eyes.

Apparently satisfied with his observations, he stopped speaking and there was an uncomfortable pause, which went on way too long. I glanced at Mark, whose face was completely expressionless and realised that after Peter's tactless blunder, Mark had stalled. He couldn't say that Claire was dead.

It came to me in a rush, this whole evening, the extravagant hugs for Mark, the slightly forced conversation at table, it was because this was the first time he had seen most of these people since the funeral, maybe before. Despite his inherent, impeccable, good manners, the evening had been the equivalent of running the gauntlet for him.

I only knew the Mark I saw since we'd met, but suddenly I was confronted by his past. He'd had a whole other life, had been intending to travel on a completely different path to the one he was on now. At least we had that in common and I felt his pain. I stepped into the widening silence to rescue Mark, "We were just going to get some drinks, Peter. Mark, will you get me a glass of water please. I'll stay and have a chat."

Mark, still looking a bit waxen, marshalled himself and walked towards the bar where I could see Dom with Vale and a few others. I turned back to my drunken companion, "Peter, I'm not Claire." I said firmly and clearly "Claire died a year ago, it's still very difficult for Mark."

Peter took a moment to focus on me and what I'd said. Clearly not the sharpest intellect at the best of times, alcohol had slowed his mental processing to a stately lumber.

"Died?"

"Yes, a year ago."

"Oh... put my foot in it." he said with dawning realisation.

"You have rather, Mark will be fine, he'll understand you didn't know, just give him a few moments."

Peter opened his mouth as if to say something else, then his eyes lost focus again and he wandered off rather aimlessly. I doubted he'd remember much about the incident.

Vale intercepted me on the way back towards the bar, "Ellie, Dom sent me to find you, are you driving back? Mark's had a couple of stiff whiskeys and is getting a tad the worse for wear, Dom says he doesn't normally drink much. Would you prefer to stay at Dom's tonight or to get a hotel?"

"Oh gosh," I said "No, I can drive him back, I've got to get home for the dogs."

Hats off to Dom for recognising the signs, because apart from a slight air of concentration as he spoke, Mark didn't seem too bad to me. We said our goodbyes all round and the four of us walked back to the car. Safely belted in, Mark assured me he would direct me out of the city and looked at the A-Z. About three minutes later when I said "Left or right?", I realised his head was lolling and he was sound asleep. I defy anyone to navigate using an A-Z whilst driving, so we did our prophesied, slightly less-than-magical mystery tour around the back of Bethnal Green, because I went wrong. I finally found signs to the A12, despite my peacefully sleeping companion and drew up outside the barn about forty minutes later. I wondered how many times Claire had had to drive him home unconscious from a 'do' or whether Dom was right about him not drinking much. I hoped he stayed an affable drunk, I wasn't up for coping with any trouble. I gently shook Mark awake.

"We're back."

"Mmm?"

"Come on, last of the big drinkers, I'll let you in."

Only swaying slightly as I let him go to unlock the barn, Mark followed me inside. I made him drink a pint of water with an Alka Seltzer I'd found in the bathroom cupboard and he wandered off to bed bidding me a courteous "Goodnight."

I left a note on the side explaining that I had his car at my house, if he wanted to ring me in the morning, and drove myself home.

"Phew," I said to the dogs as I let them out "that was a night of two halves!"

As I stepped out of my red silk dress and it pooled at my feet for only the second time, the circumstances couldn't have been more different. The red dress wasn't to be a talisman for a new relationship to begin this time I thought ruefully and realised I felt disappointed. I wondered how Mark's head would be in the morning.

16. Gifts and Christmas.

"Not good." was the answer to that question! When Mark rang his voice sounded hoarse and he said he felt very fragile.

"I'll walk down this afternoon and pick up the car if that's alright with you. Ellie, I am so sorry about last night."

"Don't worry, it was a good evening... until we met Peter. Look I can see how difficult it was for you, I hadn't thought how it would be. I was a mess after Brett died, didn't go anywhere for ages because I couldn't face people. I think you were very brave to go at all."

"I can't apologise enough, you're right I didn't realise how difficult it would be for me. I think that's my first big event with the old crowd and everyone was extra specially caring, which brought it home to me. Then that great oaf Parky threw me completely. But I'm glad you were with me Ellie honestly."

"You're lucky I was, Dom was all for leaving you to walk home, but Vale and I stuck up for you and I was well rewarded, you were great company on the way back!"

"Very funny Ellie, don't tease me, my head hurts. I feel like evil goblins are hammering at my temples."

"Nice! I can drive the car up for you if you like, I'm happy to walk back."

"No, I'll walk to you, the walk will do me good, clear my head, don't worry."

"Ok I'll see you later."

When he knocked at the door, Mark looked like hell! His normally brown skin looked sallow, he had puffy bags under his eyes and a five o'clock shadow.

"Looking good." I remarked.

"It can't be worse than I feel."

"Not sure about that. Coffee? Tea? A couple of lightly poached aspirin?"

He voted for a Camomile tea and as I went to the kitchen to put the kettle on, he rifled through the Sunday paper. "What's this?" he called holding up a Christmas supplement with 'The best recipes and the best places to go for a fabulous Christmas,' earmarked.

"What's what?" I asked looking through from the kitchen door. "Oh, Mum and Dad wanted me to go down for Christmas, but the practice will be manic and I'm working Christmas Eve morning, so I wondered if they would come here instead. I was looking for recipe ideas, but got distracted, some of the country house Christmas's look amazing. I like the one in the New Forest with the carriage ride to midnight service - costs an arm and a leg though."

"I bet."

"What are you doing for Christmas?"

"Well, Dom is going to America with Vale to ski and they invited me, but I don't want to play gooseberry and anyway Mum is on her own, so I'll probably go to hers."

"Pen said that she and I should perhaps pool our parents and do something together. She always has everyone to hers and says she dreads it sometimes."

"Actually, that isn't a bad idea. Might be a bit much for Pen to cook for everyone but we could pool ours. If, well, if you don't mind? You can imagine, it might be a bit quiet just Mum and me."

"Why not?" I said warming to the idea. "I'll ask mine tonight, see what they say. It'll be a bit compact bijou in here with five of us." I said looking doubtfully round my tiny sitting room. "Will your Mum mind?"

"No, not at all, she's great my Mum, but if you like, we could do it at the barn. The rooms won't be finished, but I'll be living in there by then, everything important will work, what do you think?"

"Done!" I said. "I can still do the dinner though, I'll have to get Mum to do a Christmas pudding and some mince pies at the very least or she'll be flapping about not doing anything. Perhaps you and your Mum could do the nibbles, extra bits and cheese? Actually, it'll be fun, I didn't fancy going down to them on my own."

When Pen heard about it, she said she would be having words with Mark about stealing her idea and her guests, but asked us to join them for Christmas evening instead. "We play silly games like charades and grown-up pass the parcel. We can drink sloe gin, it’ll dull the pain."

I was looking forward to Christmas more than I had done for years. December was always chaotic in the practice, everyone wants to be right for Christmas and there is always a rush for appointments as people start to panic. On the other hand, everyone is busy with last minute jobs and lots of parties too, so appointments get cancelled and swapped all over the place as well. Christmas Eve was upon us and the phone hadn't stopped all morning.

I'd already had a dance injury from someone who'd partied in high heels they never normally wear, with a swollen knee. A lady with a raging tennis elbow from carrying mountains of carrier bags around the shops, weighed down like a pack donkey, and someone who'd fallen off a ladder doing the decorations. The truth is, we all rush around like headless chickens and accidents happen.

I'd been busy since seven-thirty that morning and thankfully we were getting towards the end of the list. Rose put her hand over the phone and looked at me, "Can you fit one more in Ellie?"

She had fielded all the desperate pleas and worked miracles, managing the diary with military precision to fit people in all week and we were both on our knees.

"Is it really urgent?" I had to pick up the turkey before the Butcher closed at two o'clock and it was twelve thirty already.

"He says 'yes'. A terrible headache apparently."

"Oh crikey, Rose, I suppose I'd better see him."

Headaches can be hiding other more serious issues and I felt I ought to do a triage at least, to see if he needed to go to A&E. Several people had been added to my list already that morning and as I showed him into the treatment room it was nearly twenty past one.

Mr Brown, was short with receding blonde hair and a slightly peeved expression. I started my normal assessment with him about his headache, where it was and what type of symptoms he had. He described in some detail a fairly classical pattern of headache referring upwards from the top of the neck and spreading across one side of his scalp to the eye. His stooped posture with a poked-out chin and a sharp hinge across the centre of his neck at the back, rather than a nice smooth neck curve certainly suggested that the neck joints may be compressed and overloaded and could be the source of his pain. It was when I asked what had caused his headache today, that he dropped his bombshell.

"Oh, it didn't start today - I've had headaches like these for years - I was off work this morning and thought it would be nice if you could sort it for me for Christmas!"

I wasn't quite sure what to say, he clearly didn't see anything amiss with keeping us all at the clinic late at Christmas on a whim. Thoughts of my turkey being locked into the butchers and us having a vegetarian Christmas sprang to mind, but in the end, I said nothing, what was the point?

I did ease his symptoms a little with treatment and explained that we could probably sort this out more permanently if he would come in for a short course of treatment after Christmas. He declined any further appointments saying that he normally attended Martin's clinic, but that Martin hadn't been able to fit him in being Christmas Eve. He paid and left without even wishing us a Merry Christmas.

After he left, Rose said "Is everything alright? You look as if all your feathers are ruffled, like an indignant bird."

"Some people are the dizzy limit, Rose."

I was worried about getting everything ready for Mark's mum and I wanted it to be right, for some reason I didn't want her or him for that matter, to think I was useless. I had a vision of a serene Claire whisking up amazing things in the kitchen, whilst looking effortlessly beautiful and probably being Mark's mum's best friend to boot. Editing my unworthy thoughts, I explained to Rose what had happened with Mr Brown... She was about to say something pithy, but in the end, we had to laugh.

"It says more about him than it does about us," she said wisely "we did the right thing."

"I suppose so", I said grudgingly. "They deserve each other."

"Look though, Trish brought in a Poinsettia for you and there is an exciting looking package from Louise. Lots of people have brought in biscuits and chocolates this morning, on their way past, so we're lucky, most of our patients are great."

"You're so right Rose, they are. Come on, let's lock up, before anyone else rings, Christmas begins here."

I ran to my car and stowed the plant and my gifts safely, then set sail for the Butcher where hopefully my turkey still awaited me. I arrived at five past two and the door was locked. My heart sank. There was still a light on at the back and I walked round to the yard at the back of the shop and called out "Helloo."

Joe, the Butcher, appeared his striped apron smeared with blood and said "We was gettin' worried about you Ellie, I says to Dave we'd have to drop it in to Pen's on the way 'ome, that or eat it ourselves!"

"I'm so sorry, I got held up at work - last minute emergencies."

"It's been manic here too, we've been up all night doing the orders, just sitting down with a cuppa tea before we clear up, you like one Ellie?"

"I'd love one." I said and sank down onto an upturned crate accepting the big mug gratefully.

On my way home, my thoughts turned to gifts and Christmas. There were wrapped boxes and tree presents in the sitting room ready for tomorrow. I had gifts in the car from old and new patients. Friends and family to share the day with tomorrow, I was lucky, Mr Brown was the exception.

Gifts from patients have been many and varied over the years. The most unusual, yet touchingly thoughtful, was the cut off legs of some Pyjama trousers in a brown paper bag. When handed it, my clearly bemused expression on opening the bag, prompted my patient Doris to explain-

"The pyjamas you told me about last treatment, the ones that the elastic made you itch... well I was shortening some of my pyjamas and I thought you could use the cut off legs to re-cover your waistband, so the elastic doesn't touch your skin."

Clearly her faith in my sewing capabilities outstripped my own and at that moment, a great chasm opened between us, filled with the weight of expectation and erroneously perceived like-mindedness. In the face of her confidence, I could not admit my complete aversion to all things needlework. The amputated pyjama legs still reproach me from the bottom of my sewing basket.

The most mysterious gift I have ever received, was a small square box with a faded damask covering, in shades of turquoise and cream. A tiny, smooth bone shard on a ribbon attached to the lid, fed through a ribbon loop on the body of the box to make a simple clasp. Bill the owner, had one of the worst backs and arthritic knees I have ever seen. Bent over now and stiff, he walked with wide stance and a rocking gait, his knees bowed outward alarmingly. He had been a car mechanic, when they thought nothing of slinging a rope over a tree and pulling an engine out single handed. He had worked outside in all weathers and was a regular customer, particularly in the cold weather. Bill handed me the box and as he did, a slightly damp smell pervaded, as if it had been secreted away and only just re-discovered. I opened the stiff cardboard lid and was surprised to feel a velvety cushioning beneath it. But as I looked at the contents of the box the reason for its presence became clear. A tiny porcelain pot nestled inside, its miniature lid concealed congealed, red wax. Beside the pot lay a smooth, cold finger of marble with Chinese characters engraved in relief on the circular base.

"How lovely!" I exclaimed, "a seal."

"Well," he said "It belonged to my Grandfather, don't rightly know where he got it. He said he won it playing Ma Jong down near the docks in Limehouse from a Chinese sailor, but me Grandad was always telling tall tales. I never knew what to do with it and well, you do all that Chinesey stuff, don't you?"

Bill was referring to my Acupuncture training during which we learnt to do any amount of "Chinesey" stuff. The fob and wax were beautiful and I loved the yin and yang of the set, soft cushion/ hard marble, warm wax/cold fob, decorative box/functional purpose.

"So, I wanted you to have it, thought it might mean something to you." Bill continued, "I loved me Grandad and he couldn't abide things that were made to be used, sitting in cupboards doing nothing."

"Bill, it's beautiful," I replied, "I shall treasure it." I could see it sitting on my office desk. I would enjoy the feel of the cold marble fob. When I was concentrating, I tended to play with something, and I could imagine rolling the smooth stone in my palm, like Greek worry beads. I could use it to seal letters sometimes too. I wasn’t sure what the inscription meant, but in my mind, I would be sealing my correspondence with the love Bill had for his Grandad and the thoughtfulness he showed me.

When I arrived home, the cottage was all quiet. I squeezed through the front door with all my bags, kicking it shut behind me. The tiny sitting room exuded its habitual cosy welcome and two sets of paws with smiley heads popped up over the half door to the kitchen. "Hi Guys." I said as I worked my way past the dogs into the kitchen to put the Turkey in the fridge. Birdie tried to edge her nose into the carrier bag as I passed her.

"Leave it." I said, "Maybe some scraps tomorrow... If you're good."

I opened the back door, let the dogs out into the garden then clicked the kettle on, I had time for a quick sandwich before everyone arrived and the festivities got underway. I'd just got the first mouthful in, when the phone rang. I walked into the sitting room to answer, it was a slightly breathless Mum,

"Oh Darling, it's only me, we have stayed longer at Jack and Anne's than we expected, so just leaving now. We'll be with you about five thirty, six-ish depending on the traffic."

"That’s fine Mum, no problem, see you soon, drive safely."

I put the phone back in the cradle and felt quite relieved, that took the pressure off a bit.

Grabbing a notepad by the phone, I made a quick list of what I needed to do today, then a second list for Christmas day. It’s only a posh roast dinner, but with everything else going on, if I wrote a quick plan to glance at, I wouldn’t forget things. I sometimes think that writing things down fixes what I've got to do in my brain too. Brett used to add things to the bottom of my lists like *Don't forget to make another list.* He thought my lists were hilarious. I felt better with it down on paper, less stuff buzzing round my head.

I checked my watch, about two hours before anyone arrived, that gave me time to go to the Barn quickly to do some decorating, then walk the dogs. I transferred six festive, red, poinsettia's, bought earlier in the week from the local garden centre, from the kitchen to the seat-well of the car. I added a large bin bag full of tendrils of ivy from my garden and some red-berried holly. A large roll of scarlet ribbon and some scissors were added, then, grabbing the spare key Mark had given me, I rugged up in a thick tweed jacket and wellies and loaded the dogs into their crate at the back of the car.

I let myself into the barn and set about making bunches of holly and ivy tied with trailing red ribbon bows and hung them around the room. I trailed more ivy over the door frames and stacked Poinsettias around the hearth with one for the centre of the long refectory table. The room looked rustic but festive as I stepped back to judge the effect. I felt pleased with my handiwork. I let myself back out and gave the dogs a good run over the farm fields in the half-light before returning home, cheeks stinging and rosy from the sharp December cold. I could make out the warm glow of light in Pen's kitchen across the field and imagined her up to her elbows in flour, baking and singing Christmas songs.

Still no sign of my Parents, so I set about making our traditional Christmas Eve fish pie. Chunks of salmon and white fish with scallops, prawns and hard-boiled eggs all in a creamy white sauce with lashings of fluffy mash browned in the oven. I was almost done when Jeeves started to bark and the headlights of Mum and Dad's car shone through the front window. Taking precautions to move everything tasty out of the dog's reach, I went to let them in, laughing at Mum bustling and directing Dad and at him giving me a slightly baleful and resigned smile. I hugged them both, helped Dad with the bags, amid familiar half caught sentences.

"Traffic so bad, still it is Christmas Eve."

"Never can get away from Jack and Anne's on time..."

"Your Mother has brought half the house!"

"I've put you up in my room, just be careful on the stairs they are so steep, especially after a few of Jack's sherries Mother."

After all the commotion of the arrival and a cup of tea, I suggested we eat around seven o'clock then pop up to the farm to say hello to Mark and his Mum. I'd been feeling nervous about how everyone would get on, so I hoped they would agree and not be too tired, I wanted to break the ice before the big day. Perhaps if everyone was still on their feet, we could go to Midnight service in the village church after, it was so pretty. Maybe Mark's Mum wasn't religious or maybe she would want to go to her own church... I suddenly realised how much I didn't know about his family and panicked that this arrangement may go horribly wrong.

Replete with fish pie, we set off for the Barn about eight thirty. It was a still night, sharply cold and we huddled into our coats and gloves, misty breath preceding us as we walked out to the car. I briskly scraped a light frost that had spangled the windscreen with ice crystals and jumped into the car. It barely had time to warm up on the short journey and I could feel my face getting chilled as I drove.

We knocked on the barn door and Mark came to greet us an enticing aroma of spiced oranges and cinnamon wafting from a glass of mulled wine in his hand.

"Come in, come in!"

I did the introductions- "My Mum and Dad - Graham and Susan - this is my friend Mark."

He shook Dad's hand and gave Mum a kiss on each cheek, which took her by surprise and made her blush. Then he kissed me on the cheek and said "Cold nose Ellie! Come in and meet my Mother... Mama this is Ellie and her Parents - Graham and Susan - my Mother Alessandra." Nice company manners I noted and blessed him for being so welcoming.

Dark haired with the same olive skin as Mark, Alessandra was an elegant lady. She had Mark's eyes, a wide generous mouth and the same dark curly hair, although as she wore hers long, it fell in deep waves as opposed to his tousled mop of curls. She retained just a hint of an accent in her low-pitched voice which made her seem slightly exotic. In a photo I had seen, Alessandra looked like a slightly finer-boned version of Sophia Loren, but in real life she was less languid and exuded grace and vivacity. I had a momentary panic and felt a quick knotting in my stomach as I glanced at Mum. With slightly over-permed hair, no make-up and a floral dress chosen more for the fact it was washable than for its sartorial merits, I wondered how would these two women get on and more to the point, was Mum going to be judgmental and do her tight lipped, disapproving politeness trick!

"Good to see you, come in, we are drinking hot punch and getting a little bit tipsy." Alessandra giggled.

Mark took our coats and asked "Anyone for a glass of mulled wine or something else?"

I held my breath, was Mum going to approve and join in or was she going to stiffly ask for a cup of tea and go all Quakerish...

"No, no, no!" Alessandra cut in "you sort out Ellie and Graham. Susan and I will get our own drinks thank you." Then as an aside to Mum she said "I like an extra tot of cherry brandy in my mulled wine, these youngsters are such lightweights!"

I held my breath, there was an infinitesimal pause where everything hung in the balance between the two women, but Alessandra had her, Mum's desire for some of the Hollywood glamour of the 1940's movies that she loved, won out over the sensible housewife. Alessandra had deftly charmed her into being an ally!

We sat round the fire cupping glasses of mulled wine and getting to know each other. Alessandra was very chatty and even had my Father - well known monosyllabic at parties, at ease, joking and laughing, with Mum joining in. I felt reassured, it boded well for the day tomorrow.

Time slipped away and glancing at my watch, I said "I'm sorry to break up the party, but If we're going to get a seat at Midnight service, we should think about heading off."

"Would you drop me back to the cottage on the way," said Mum "I'm think I'm too tired and too comfortable to stay awake for Midnight service."

"Me too." Dad agreed.

I dropped them back at the Cottage and headed to the old village church on my own. As I drove along deserted roads, the houses in the town nestled squat and cosy behind back-lit, coloured curtains and twinkly outside lights. I wondered how excited the children inside the homes were and what family traditions and preparations were underway. I'd always thought that Brett and I would have kids of our own by now, they'd have been a harum-scarum bunch I thought, and we'd have been having Christmas at the beach if we'd still been in Australia.

The old Norman church was a perfect traditional setting for Midnight Mass, one of my favourite services of the year. I took my place in one of the carved wooden pews, polished to a rich shine, and noticed lots of familiar faces from the Practice and the town. I sang the carols I have been singing since I first remember Christmas, listened again to the familiar messages of hope in the service and then as everyone left calling out merry greetings, felt their joyful anticipation of the days to come. The midnight-blue stillness outside was serene and peaceful. I stopped for a moment, looking up at the stars, cold nipping my cheeks, and let the tranquillity of the night fill my soul. Brett was out there somewhere looking down, making part of the ether and the thought, as always, comforted me. If he had still been alive, where would I have been this Christmas?

"I still miss you," I whispered, "why did you have to go and get killed you idiot!"

"No good crying over spilt milk," my Nan would have said, so I brushed away the tear that had spilt down my cheek as I blinked and headed for my trusty car, which smelt of the dogs and was mine not ours.

I drove home and crept into the house, as quietly as anyone can who owns Gordon Setters and unrolled my sleeping bag. Suddenly, I felt drained and couldn't be bothered with the pump-up mattress, so snuggled in on the sofa. Unwanted thoughts of everything that needed to be done tomorrow and what might have been, were firmly discarded and I drifted off into the deep and dreamless sleep of the exhausted.

I woke the following morning just a little stiff from the cramped position on the sofa, shuffled sleepily into the kitchen and let the dogs out. I saw that cloud cover had come in overnight, so Christmas morning dawned grey and overcast. My Parents, who had waited only for signs of life from me to come down, made their slightly creaky way down my killer stairs saying "Merry Christmas," "Happy Christmas Darling," and Dad enveloped me in a hug while Mum put the kettle on. The failure of the weather to meet text book expectations did not dampen our spirits as we drank tea and ate smoked salmon and scrambled egg with bagels. It was all so familiar, our tried and tested Christmas rituals and they were beyond pleased to be here, it would have been churlish to be wishing myself elsewhere and I surrendered to the comfort of well-worn rituals. We discussed what we needed to take with us and after quick showers, we collected everything together in the sitting room. As we ferried it all to the car, Dad mock grumbled "It's only one day." We decided to exchange our presents when we got there, so they were squeezed in as well and we set off for the Barn.

Our day with Mark and Alessandra turned out to be special in an understated sort of way, despite my concerns. It wasn't a mad party, but a comfortable, friendly day full of tender moments. After the initial unloading and finding a space for everything, we all agreed a cup of coffee would be good, and hugging our mugs, we settled around the island in the kitchen and started to prepare the vegetables.

"Did you enjoy Sarah's wedding?" Alessandra asked as she inspected a large potato for any residual eyes.

Mark shot me a quick glance and for a moment I teased him with my return look, before replying "We had a lovely evening thank you, Mark's a secret dancer, so we strutted our stuff to the swing band."

"I taught her everything she knows," said my Dad.

"Flipping cheek," I said giving him a push "what about all those dance lessons in the village hall?"

"We won the parent and child prize two years running if I remember rightly...?"

"You did too," said Mum "and you so wanted one of those dresses your dance teacher made and I was too mean to buy one and made you wear one that Nan had altered for you."

"I have never got over it" I said shaking my head.

"I think this calls for a demonstration" said Alessandra.

We ended up pushing back the island and whilst Mum beat time with a potato peeler pinafore in place over her Christmas frock, Alessandra hummed a tune and Dad danced a waltz with me, him in his slippers and me in my stocking feet. I love my Dad.

Somehow, between the five cooks and a fair bit of reminiscing, we managed to produce a fine Christmas dinner and enjoyed it, toasting our culinary skill and teamwork. We had just a passing moment of sadness as we toasted "Absent Friends". Welcoming our sadness to the feast, rather than pretending it didn't exist, seemed to draw us together and I no longer felt the raw pain of loss I had, even last year. I realised it was four years since Brett died and wondered with a sudden panic if he was slipping away from me completely. Catching Mark's eye, I saw he too had a fleeting moment of pain. As we acknowledged each other's feelings, there was a genuine warmth in our exchanged glance, we weren't just two bereaved souls sharing memories anymore, we had truly become good friends and had new memories to add to the old. Memories made together, with new friends, in our new lives. The toast wasn't solely for ghosts though, Dom and

Vale, Pen and Angus, extended family and other friends were all brought momentarily to the table.

Invited to Pen and Angus for seven that evening, we in fact, didn't get there as planned. A small drama occurred in the shape of a four-legged thief...

No one could manage cheese and biscuits after the main meal, so I covered them, leaving them on the side along with a basket of mandarins and grapes. I thought nothing of it, until I glanced into the kitchen and saw Bird eating something. "What have you got?" I said and went to investigate. All that was left of the bunch of grapes was a stalk! Grapes are so toxic to dogs, that emergency action ensued. I phoned through to the out of hours vet and thanking my stars that I stuck with soft drinks at lunchtime because of the drive home, put Bird in the car. I made my lonely way to Witham on still deserted roads, apparently the only brave souls not asleep in front of the television were me and the vet on duty!

Treatment was not pretty... poor Bird (naughty Bird!) was injected to make her sick and having checked that the grapes were not digested, she was put on a drip in case her kidneys had been affected by the toxin. I had to leave her overnight, under observation in the vet hospital. She looked extremely sorry for herself as I left. Wending my way back to the Barn, I kicked myself for not being more careful, I normally put everything well out of the dog's reach in the kitchen. It made an anxious end to an otherwise lovely day.

Everyone wanted all the gory details over a last cup of tea and after explanations to the assembled company, we parted with promises to let Mark and Alessandra know how Bird was as soon as I had news. My cottage seemed all wrong with just Jeeves there, not helped by the fact he was clearly searching for Birdie and kept whining and asking to go out to check the garden. I finally insisted he came in and settled.

I remembered my stiffness after a night on the sofa last night, so I bothered to inflate the air bed and broke the rules by letting Jeeves sleep beside me. His soft warmth was comforting and he seemed even more precious all of a sudden.

I was relieved the next day to be told Bird seemed fine, with normal blood test results and that she could come home on the 27th if all continued well. I phoned everyone to let them know and we let out a collective held breath. The call put Christmas back in the happy zone, but my bank balance less so, four hundred pounds! Thank goodness for pet insurance.

We walked the very lonely Jeeves over the footpaths towards the farm on Boxing day morning and popped into Pen and Angus to say sorry for letting them down the night before.

"Don't apologise Ellie, what a horrible thing - I can't believe Birdie did that, she isn't usually a counter surfer."

"I know and I'm usually so careful, thank goodness she's OK, I'll be more careful in future."

Pen gave me a hug and said "Don't beat yourself up too much, it was an accident... Look, I was wondering, would you like to stay for some lunch? We have so much food left over. Do you think if I give Mark and his Mum a call, they may wander over too?"

I glanced at Mum and Dad to see what they thought, but they seemed quite relaxed at the prospect, so we agreed. Pen went off to see what Mark and Alessandra were doing. They said they would walk over to join us, so Pen and I set about carving cold meat, laying the table and loading it with pickles, cheese and salad. Whilst we were busy, my Dad made his signature bubble and squeak with the left-over potatoes, onions, bacon and sprouts all pan fried crisp and golden. It's a Rose household classic and part of Dads limited repertoire in the kitchen. Pen and Angus had been too full up for their Christmas pudding yesterday, so Mum put that in a pan on the Aga to steam and made custard to go with it. Our combined efforts put another tasty lunch on the table. Picking at all the leftovers on Boxing day is sometimes better than the main meal at Christmas.

The impromptu party didn't break up until early evening, by which time it was too dark to walk back over the fields, so Pen offered to take us home.

Alessandra was leaving the next day, as she was flying to relatives in Italy for New Year, so it was time to say goodbye for now. We had such a good time together, that she suggested we might all meet in London one day to have lunch and see a show. She also extended an invitation to come to see her down in Surrey, for a weekend when the weather was better. So often these "holiday" plans to re-meet never amount to much but I felt we would do both, Alessandra was warm and funny and I'd like to see her again. As we stepped out into the cold, she wrapped me in a huge hug and whispered in my ear "Thank you my darling girl, he has been so unhappy and there is a glimmer of his old self back."

It was lucky she moved on quickly to Mum and Dad, because I had no idea what to say in reply.

17. The start of the year.

After so much fun at Christmas, January fell a little flat. The short, cold days were relentlessly wet and miserable with low grey clouds and biting winds. Pen and I continued to walk and train the dogs, on sodden fields, so we and the dogs came back coated in mud every day. They were very fed up with their daily shower, I was sick of washing dirty bedding and the smell of wet dog! I felt restless and bored. Although Dom and Vale were back from skiing, they had stayed up in London and the windows of the Barn remained dark, as Mark too was away on business.

"I think you're missing Mark, Ellie." Said Pen, as we and the dogs sat against her Aga trying to get warm after one freezing walk.

"No, I'm not, trust you! It's not that, I hate January it's so gloomy, there is always more month than money and Spring isn't even around the corner."

“Ellie, you’re such a fibber, I saw you looking at the barn longingly when we were on the fields.”

“I was not!”

“Hmm, why won’t you give Mark a chance?”

“Oh Pen, I really like him, and he can look very handsome too, but he can be a bit moody and he blows hot and cold. Sometimes I think he is interested and then I’m not sure. I don’t think he’s over Claire yet and I’m not sure I can cope with that. I can’t compete with a dead wife.

“He has to though, compete with a dead saint.”

“Pen that’s a terrible thing to say, Brett wasn’t a saint but he was my absolute soulmate. Look, for your information, Mark he has never asked me on a date, unless you can call the drunken wedding debacle a date. Anyway, I don’t know if I have got time for a relationship, with all that’s going on at work.

”I think you’re scared to try Ellie. Mark’s Mum thinks you’d make a good pair, so does Angus.”

“Good to know we’re a hot topic of conversation! When were you talking to Alessandra about me?” I felt defensive and hurt, Pen could be so bossy and pushy sometimes.

“On Boxing Day, she asked me if I thought you might fall for each other and I said I thought you might - if you weren’t such a stubborn workaholic who couldn’t see past the end of your nose.”

“Pen, you are joking? I am not stubborn and if you had a business to keep going when the economy’s falling about your ears and you may go bust, you might be a workaholic too. Oh my goodness, you haven’t said any of this to Mark have you?”

Hideous scenes of him feeling smug and laughing about me with Dom came to mind, or worse him cringing with embarrassment at Pen and his Mum trying to push us together. “Pen you haven’t?”

“Oh keep your wool on, neither of us has said anything.”

Suddenly, all that Pen had said in exasperation seemed too much, I was angry and I stood up abruptly, "I need to go, I'm sorry Pen but please don't talk about me to Mark's Mum, I don't know how I'm ever going to face her again or him for that matter."

"Don't be like that Ellie, we were only trying to help. You've both been so lonely..."

"Come on dogs" I said a bit more sharply than I'd intended, they both shot to my side, looking slightly apprehensive. "It's not you." I muttered

"Ellie don't go like this."

But I was already heading for the door, tears of what? Anger, self-pity, humiliation, pricking at my eye-lids.

I slumped on the sofa when I got home seething with resentment and watched the news. I wished I hadn't, there was little in the news to cheer anyone up. The storms at the start of the Month had left a death toll and carnage in their wake, and there was talk of us going to war in Iraq. More bad news about recession followed and I was seriously worried about how the hike in interest rates had hit my business loan repayments already and they seemed set to keep steadily climbing. People didn't understand about Touch, it seemed like everything was going well and it was in terms of how many patients I was seeing, but, even though I was working as hard as I could, the outgoings on the loan repayments were getting very high and I wondered how long I could keep running if the costs continued to rise? People were handing the keys to their homes back to mortgage companies every day, I felt so frightened this economic situation would swallow my business whole, and I realised how important a part of me it had become. Somehow it was the symbol of survival since Brett died. And now Pen was telling me to forget him, I felt so hurt.

Pen phoned later to apologise for upsetting me, I knew it wasn't all her fault, she'd touched a raw nerve and I still felt bruised. I tried to reassure her that it was OK and I was just tired, but I could hear in her voice she didn't think I'd forgiven her and she was probably right.

The next day I found a tin on my step with a huge fruit cake and a note "Sorry Hun, Angus says I'm a tactless idiot, Pen xx."

I looked at the tin and smiled, cake? So like Pen. I felt myself soften, we'd never had a row before. I picked up the tin, "Why not? Might as well get fat too," I said to the dogs as I stepped inside. I would make my peace with Pen later.

A week after Pen and I had fallen out in her kitchen, I had a call from Mike Neville, the trainer from when we had been awarded our Gundog Working Certificates. It was the news we had been hoping for, but it couldn't have come at a worse time. I phoned Pen.

"We've done it!"

"Slow down Ellie - done what?"

"Just had a call from Mike Neville - he's asked us to go counting with him, with the dogs in Yorkshire."

"Really?" She squeaked "That's fantastic Ellie, just brilliant!"

"Yep, he has a new piece of moorland he has been asked to count the ground-nesting birds on, so we're invited to join him at the end of March, if we can make it."

"Make it? Are you kidding? This is what we've been waiting for." She squeaked.

“Pen you may have to go on your own. I know it’s what we’ve been training for, but I don’t think I can afford to take the time off at the moment.”

“Ellie, don’t be silly, of course you must come too, you need a break, everything has been so stressful and one week off is not going to change the grand scheme of things.”

“I don’t know, I need to think about it.”

I should have known better than to think Pen would leave it at that, in the evening I had a call from Mark, who was still away on business. “Ellie, how are things? Pen rang me, she’s worried you might be getting a bit burnt-out, we all are. Why don’t you plan to take the break she told me about in Yorkshire. It might make things clearer if you got away for a week. Look let me take a look at the business with you, if you’re really worried, it’s what I do best...”

Why is it that when someone suggests what you’ve been thinking about you suddenly clam up? I had wondered about asking for Mark’s professional advice, now perversely, I didn’t want him to tell me that Touch was struggling and after what Pen had said about us falling for each other, I felt embarrassed, I didn’t want him thinking I was a lovestruck idiot.

“She shouldn’t have rung you Mark, I’m really sorry, I don’t know what’s the matter with her lately.”

“We’re just worried that you’re working so hard, we hardly see you. Sometimes taking a step back helps get everything in perspective.”

“Well its nice of you to be concerned but I’m sure I’ll muddle through. Thank you for the offer.”

As soon as I put the phone down, I realised I’d been a bit off with him, he was trying to help. But really, all of them fussing and talking about me! Worst of all, I could hear Brett saying "That wasn't very gracious of you Ellie, why don't you let go your pride and accept some help?"

"I don't know why," I shouted at his memory, "Because you're not here and I have to be able to manage alone or I'll sink; because I can't bear Mum to do her '*Well women just aren't cut out for business like men are.*' speech; because I will not have horrible Martin with his awful practice gloating if I go under." But I was shouting to thin air and promptly burst into tears.

When I was all cried out, I had to admit Mark could be right about taking a break, it's what I would have told a patient to do. It wasn't like me to be bursting into tears all over the place or falling out with Pen. The prospect of getting in the car and driving North, leaving money worries, man troubles and general misery behind, suddenly seemed very inviting. Of course, it would be amazing to see that all our training with the dogs in the fields and on courses had not been in vain. I wanted to see the dogs doing some real work too.

Mark got back soon after his phone call and he came to see me, looking slightly like he wasn't sure of his welcome. I told him I'd taken his advice and was going to do the counting and talked about it at some length, to stop him asking about the business. Poor chap struggled to get a word in edgeways to tell me why he had popped in. Alessandra true to her promise that we should meet in London, had organised tickets to see Phantom of the Opera, which had had such brilliant reviews and was the hot ticket. Alessandra had invited Dom and Vale too. We all met at the Shaftesbury Theatre the following Friday evening. Dom clearly loved Alessandra and enveloped her in a bear hug then held her at arms-length looking her up and down and said "Beautiful and elegant as always."

"Flatterer." She said with ill-concealed pleasure.

"This is Vale," he said drawing her forward and then linked arms with both, "let me buy you both a drink, you will be such friends I know. Ellie, I have no arms left, but I can recommend Mark as an excellent chap! Come on Mark chop, chop, they will be five-deep at the bar before we get there."

Mark looked at me and smiled offering his arm in imitation and we followed in their wake, me wondering how many more people were in the plot to throw Mark and I together. Dom over-did the charm in a flagrant way all evening, but he did it with such style and humour, he had a knack of making everyone feel special. Alessandra dropped no broad hints about Mark and I, Mark was good company but was clearly steering clear of my thorns and I ended up relenting and relaxing into their good company.

If Mark had put a foot wrong, I could have consigned him to the 'friend only' bin and solved one of my problems, but he was irritatingly word perfect and I almost relented and told him all my troubles. Almost.

The buzz of excitement in the theatre foyer was palpable as we threaded through the crowd and up the carpeted stairs. We had only just finished our drinks when the three-minute ball rang and we took our seats as an expectant hush fell in the auditorium and the orchestra began to play...

"Breath-taking!"

"So beautiful - the staging was fantastic."

"Wow, amazing."

The superlatives were flying all around us as we made our way out after the performance. It had been hauntingly beautiful from start to finish and I felt a little displaced as I was dragged from that world back into this.

"Did you enjoy it?" Mark asked.

"Wonderful." I said and turning to Mark's Mum "Thank you so much for getting the tickets."

Despite all the grim news around us, the upcoming holiday and the lovely evening out gave me a short reprieve.

18. Pam.

Sadly, February started with an unexpected phone call from Pam Bane that wiped out that small reprieve.

"Ellie, can you take a look at my back. I've got a horrible pain between my shoulder blades and I can't seem to shift it."

"Yes, come on in, I have a slot tomorrow if you can make it, will 10.45 suit you?"

"Yes, I can make that, I'll see you then, can't wait actually."

As I asked Pam into the treatment room, I was struck by how much slimmer she was, curiously, she was wearing the suit she'd worn to her first appointment at the breast unit and it looked way too big for her now. The skirt waist had settled onto her hips so that the shaping wasn't in the right place and the jacket looked hollow.

"Wow" I said "you're looking svelte."

"I know, all my clothes are a bit big now, I must buy some more, I think the tablets may be affecting me, I haven't been dieting."

"So, what has happened to your back Pam?" I asked.

"I honestly don't know, it started up gradually, just after the Charity tea party for MacMillan about six weeks ago. I thought I must've overdone it, moving tables and lifting the urn - we made two hundred and fifteen pounds by the way."

"Well done you. Do you think you pulled your back then?"

"Well not really, but it's all I can think of."

"Does anything particular stir the pain up?"

"Well certainly bending, even if I'm bending over my desk writing or looking down to do the ironing. The worst thing is, I can't get comfy in bed. I've started sleeping in the spare room so I don't disturb Peter."

"Can you get into a comfy position at all to ease it off?"

"Once it starts there isn't one. I have to resort to painkillers. I think I've trapped a nerve. Oh, by the way, I am still using your relaxation cassette Ellie, it's addictive, I can drift away to a good place and escape the pain."

Usually mechanical pain, the sort you get with a stiff joint or a torn muscle, allows you to find some supported position that eases the pain. It's inflammatory pain that doesn't change with positioning and is often bad at night or which persists even when the area seems offloaded. Don't get me wrong, some mechanical pain, when it's acute, can have inflammatory components to it, so this is not a black and white issue. However, inflammatory pain can have more sinister connotations of underlying pathology such as inflammatory arthritis and cancer. Given Pam's recent history of breast cancer, her sudden weight loss and her pain pattern, I was feeling rather worried. Breast cancers sometimes spread to the bones. I made my usual physical assessment and came up rather short of indicators for mechanical pain, no obvious joint stiffness, no tenderness in the muscles and no signs of a trapped nerve. Nothing really added up.

"Pam, I'm going to send you back to the doctor to get some pain meds so you can sleep properly and I'd like you to have an x-ray or scan on this before we decide on any treatment."

"That's fine Ellie," she said looking at me gravely. The elephant in the room was that the cancer could be back and we both knew it.

I didn't wait to write, I phoned through to Pam's doctor and managed to speak to him at lunchtime. I felt this needed to be checked as quickly as possible. He agreed and fast tracked the tests.

I so wanted to be wrong for this lovely lady, but I had a feeling I wasn't. The day the results were due, I set aside time in the afternoon and popped in to Wisteria Cottage. Pam and Peter were in the kitchen. Peter looked ashen but offered me tea, moving around the kitchen in a semblance of normality that was part automatic, part to reassure himself. Pam was more matter of fact.

"You knew, didn't you?"

"I suspected."

"The cancer has spread into my bones, it's not good Ellie, I have shadows all over my scan, but an especially large one where my back pain is - if that vertebra collapses, I could be paralysed. They think I have six months. Six months isn't long is it? I can't really take it in. I'm not scared, well not yet, I may be later. I suppose all sorts of things change from day to day."

Pam was not to be one of the lucky ones, one of the increasing number of women and men who survive breast cancer. I was sad for her and her family of course, sad for our community too, every community needs their Pam. Sad for myself, I was extremely fond of her, admired her ability to keep doing small things that make a real difference to people. She would never make the headlines, but in her own way she was a heroine.

Pam did not have six months, she didn't even have six weeks - only four. I carried on seeing Pam at home, helped alongside her medical treatment with pain relief, relaxation and by offering a space where it was alright not to be brave. Why do people with cancer have to fight bravely? It seems an added burden to an already onerous situation. Sometimes from the outside, all we can do to help is to be present, to bear witness and share, the time for doing is over. In her last days, care passed to the palliative care team at the hospice, Pam was tiny, frail and floating on a cocktail of pain relief when I saw her for the last time.

"It's time to go," she said to me.

We had always been honest with each other she and I, and so with a brief kiss on her cheek, all I could reply was, "Safe journey Pam."

I turned into the drive of my cottage with a heavy heart, Peter's raw grief as he sat with his wife, brought back the pain I'd felt after Brett died without warning. I opened the door and walked inside, tears running down my cheeks and slumped onto the sofa, Jeeves and Bird sensing something wrong, came up in a more subdued fashion than was usual, Bird rested her head on my lap, steadily observing me with her soft brown eyes. Jeeves hopped up beside me and as I buried my head in his soft fur, he leant in and let me cry my fill.

19. A holiday in Yorkshire.

When I phoned Pen to tell her about Pam, she immediately scooped me up, arriving unannounced and bearing me off with no argument, to eat and not be alone to brood. I was sad for Pam, but in a way, not sad that she had been spared a lot of suffering. I didn't know Peter well, but I did not envy him the difficult time of grieving and adaptation that lay ahead. I felt the weight of all the gloom press in on me and went back to my default status of managing one day at a time. Mark called on Peter which I thought was very brave and very generous. Sometimes, it is easier for people not to engage in these painful times and Mark had every excuse to avoid doing so. But I saw what real depth of character he had and remembered that, for all his moods and the times he'd made me cross, in the time I'd known him, I had never seen him shirk a responsibility.

It was a relief that after the slow start to the year, the practice was busy and I allowed that to numb my pain. Working so hard, before I went on holiday also lessened my guilt marginally about going away and leaving the Practice.

Pen and I were busy getting ready too, and in the week before we left, phone calls were numerous...

"It's like moving an army and we're only away a week!" Pen complained. "Still there is room in the cars and better to have too much than too little."

Finally, departure day came and, car packed to the gunnel's, I set off, winding my way through the Essex lanes onto the A120, the M11 and eventually onto the A1 North. There was no Mark to say goodbye to, he was away on business again. His small company was booming, as more and more businesses needed his advice in difficult times. I felt a small tingle of nervous excitement as the names went by - Eaton Scoton, Peterborough, Newark, ticking off the miles like a child counts down the Advent days to Christmas. To pass the time, I played a game in my head wondering who lived in the houses I passed and the towns, making up lives for them. At Blyth, I stopped off at the Hilltop Café to let the dogs stretch their legs, grab some petrol and have a sandwich with some tea from my flask. Then onward, North, until I turned off towards Leyburn and Jervaulx- finally we were in the Yorkshire Dales.

The sun shined in a blue sky peppered with puffball clouds. Clouds, cast kaleidoscope shadows on the fields below, as they drifted lazily on the breeze. The lush green dale spread before me, feminine, curved and voluptuous, feeding contented sheep and strutting pheasants. The intense green flesh of the dale was veined by ancient stone walls and freckled by stone farms and copses. Rising above the dale the rounded shoulders of the moors, masculine, broad and muscular, their skin of heather browned by Winter. Their bulk scarred and furrowed by the lash of wind and weather. Undaunted by years past and years to come, the moors stood solid and reassuring. I am more moved by the rounded beauty of this terrain than by the brash and thrusting drama of mountains. New life and growth burgeoned everywhere around me. Despite all the problems I had left behind me, I felt a glimmer of optimism bright and golden as the daffodils on the grass verge as I drove along the lane to the farmhouse.

I turned off the road onto a rough dirt track that lead up to the moor off which was Mike's farmhouse where the counting team stayed. Chickens and ducks ranged free on the paddocks around the house. Thank heavens for Pen's chickens, I thought, at least my dogs are pretty chicken-proof after strict "no chase" rules at her house. I parked up, slid out of the truck and walked over to the stone farm house where I knocked on the door.

"Ellie," beamed Mike as he opened the door "come in, you made it, good journey?"

"Yes, no problem. It's beautiful here."

"It is that, 'specially on a day like today, it can be bleak in the Winter. I'll give you a hand in with your things and show you your room. You're in with Pen if that's alright? Then we'll have a cup of tea."

"Can I let the dogs have a run somewhere first? They've been cooped up for a while."

"Yes of course do, just through the gate up there is a good field, all enclosed and no sheep or lambs in it yet."

Jeeves and Bird piled out of the car, eager to run and we strolled up to the field. They loved every minute of freedom after the long car journey and made the most of the new field scenting the air as it blew down wild scents from the moor and tracking rabbit scents along the grass.

As we turned back to the car, the scrunch of tyres on the road heralded the arrival of Pen. She bounced out of the car, hair escaping wildly from a lopsided ponytail and brushing a shower of crumbs from her jumper. Her broad smile beamed, as we walked back to meet her. My two dogs were thrilled to see her, doubly so when her Pointers, Daisy and Belle jumped out of the car too.

Mike laughed when he saw all our stuff...

"Have you two come for a month?"

"Planned for every eventuality - may have over done it." I confessed.

"Come on through." he said indicating a short hallway.

Our bedroom was downstairs at the back of the house down a couple of steps from the end of the hall.

"Originally, this part of the house was a cowshed that leaned to the house," he explained "but when I moved up here, I thought it would make a good guest annex. Shower and toilet are to the right."

It was simple, almost monastic with rough white walls, a heavy, old wooden wardrobe, chest of drawers and a wooden floor. It could have looked Spartan, but the floor was scattered with colourful rugs and the new windows had Wedgwood blue curtains which matched the duvets on the twin beds. It was fresh and rather beautiful. The views across the dale from the window were stunning.

Mike had worked in Banking and retired early, moving up to Yorkshire with his dogs. He bought the farm, renovated it and leased the fields to a local farmer and now worked his dogs. A good trainer, he often had Gundogs belonging to other people to train, he taught courses and also competed in field trials.

"Come back to the kitchen when you're ready, the others will be back soon and I can talk you through what we'll be doing."

As rookies, Pen and I were a bit nervous, both hoping we weren't going to muck this up and that our dogs would behave too.

"OK ready?" I said

"Yeah I reckon."

We headed back through to the kitchen, just as Mike was pouring tea for two guys in khaki green field clothes. Both men were in their fifties and looked lean with weathered faces. Graham the taller of the two had been a schoolfriend of Mikes. As he spoke, tiny white lines in an otherwise tanned face showed in a fan around his eyes where he obviously narrowed his eyes against the sun and weather. John hailed from a little village down the road. He was an artisan and worked as a carpenter as well as helping with the upkeep of the moor. His calloused hands felt rough in mine as we shook hands in greeting. They were so different to Mark and Dom, also longstanding friends. Obviously older, but with a certain confidence of men who knew who they were and had expertise in their field.

"Ellie, Pen Come in meet Graham and John - great friends of mine, we'll be doing the count together."

"Hi Ladies," said Graham, "good to meet you, what dogs have you brought?"

"Two Pointers," said Pen.

"I've got Gordon's for my sins..."

"Well you know what they say ... 'Pointers are born half trained, Setters die half trained'," said John.

"We're all Pointer men," Graham explained.

My heart sank and I must have looked a bit nervous because Mike chipped in, "Don't let them fool you, your dogs won't do anything out there that ours haven't done as well, it'll be fun. Tea, ladies?"

We both accepted a cup, and as we sipped from the steaming mugs, Mike spread a map of the moor onto the large refectory table.

"This is what we did today," he pointed out a penned square with three lines drawn in it. "It was quite a large block, so we walked out three times to cover the area, we take it in turns to run the dogs. When we're out tomorrow if your dog finds birds, keep a note as they fly up and tell me how many pairs and how many single birds you see during your run. I keep note for everyone, but if you've got a note-book as well its good practice to keep a tally yourselves."

"We'll be watching and count as well," said John "but sometimes as we're behind you, the dips in the terrain mean we don't see properly how many birds go up."

"Tomorrow we'll be further over on some higher ground, if the weather forecast is right. Wind is due to be coming south west, so we'll drive out, then we can work the dogs straight out into the wind. Meet about six-thirty if that's OK and take our time - hopefully down off the moor about three," Mike said. "If you girls don't mind, we thought we'd go down to the Dog and Gun – the pub in the village, to eat tonight, it'll save cooking and then we can take it in turns to cook each evening."

With the outline plan of the week in place we decided it was time to eat and headed for the village.

The Dog and Gun was a small stone-built pub with a profusion of daffodils carpeting the front lawn. The men had to duck to get through the door and a narrow passage led into a cosy bar with low beamed ceiling and a smell of wood smoke and beer. We sat round a square table in the corner by the mullioned bay window. the men with pints of local beer and Pen and I with a glass of cider each. The food was simple, but good and before long we had plates of steaming casserole with mountains of creamy mash on the table. Talk was of dogs long gone, sainted by the passage of time, amazing runs, clever finds, funny episodes on the moor. I drank it all in glancing at Pen – we couldn't wait to make some of our own memories.

Sunday dawned fair, the cool hazy morning slightly misted as we all emerged from a good night's sleep to let the dogs out. Mike was already at the kitchen range and the mouth-watering smell of bacon, eggs and toast filled the kitchen. The atmosphere was business-like as breakfast was served and eaten, flasks were filled, sandwiches packed and Pen appeared with a huge fruit cake in a tin to keep the worms from biting up on the moor.

Loading the dogs into the car, I pulled on three quarter boots and gators and slipped on a gilet over my checked shirt. Hair in a ponytail, tucked into a peaked cap, I checked for the umpteenth time that I had my dog whistle. On the whistle lanyard was a small screw top barrel containing antihistamine tablets. The moors are populated by adders and wasps as well as birds and the tablets could buy enough time to get to a vet or doctor if anyone was bitten. I packed a waterproof coat just in case, but it looked like being a warm, dry day. We all had copies of the map Mike had shown us last night and with a compass tucked in my backpack I felt ready. This was all so different from the world I'd left behind, I could almost fool myself that everything was fine.

Our cortege of vehicles rolled out of the farmyard in slow procession bouncing and rocking as the tyres gripped and rolled us forward over the uneven track. An occasional dull 'thunk' resonated in the truck as a small rock kicked up and hit the chassis. The track was rutted in places and the bar of heather growing in the centre of the track brushed the underside of the car like a scouring pad as the tyres settled into the ruts. The track led up over the moor and soon we had an amazing view stretching away below us to a reservoir in the dale. The dogs were alert in the back sitting up, scenting the air and fidgeting excitedly.

Mike slowed and jumped out of his car, checking the wind direction, checking for hidden rocks in the heather beside the track and then got back in and pulled his truck forward off the track, indicating to us to do the same. This was it, we were here. I grinned at Pen as we unloaded a dog each. First out for me was Bird - although younger than Jeeves she was more sensible and I felt more confident with her. We walked away from the cars into the wind and ahead was a great expanse of moor banking up to a high point on the left with a cairn on the skyline and a small stream or beck away down to the right. Taking the cairn as our first line of sight Mike said "OK Ellie you're up - set her off into the wind, we'll stop when we reach the moor wall. Work for as long as you want to, then we can each swap in." He indicated the great expanse of moor with a sweep of his arm and laughed, "plenty of room for all of us!"

Stepping forward, I dropped Bird at right angles to the wind, walked a little to the right to set her direction and said "Get on." She didn't need to be told twice and bounded off across the heather skimming the surface, her powerful muscles standing out as she reached forwards in front and drove with her back legs. A good hundred yards out, Bird turned in towards me again and galloped back setting the pattern in front of me to cover the ground as I walked forwards.

It's a thrilling sight, the dogs working in their element, sweeping side to side and covering the rough ground with barely a check. Then abruptly she came to a stop, a few feathered steps and Bird froze, half crouched, on point, nose forwards, tail stiff behind her, right front leg raised. I walked towards her and settling beside her said "find it" and clicking my fingers in a steady rhythm walked in behind her – five yards, ten, then came a sudden rush of wings and a laughing cackle as a pair of grouse lifted from the heather ahead of us. I blew a long blast on my whistle and Bird dropped into a down position.

"Good girl" I said giving her a delighted pat. I gave the signal to continue a short search around the area where the birds had flown from to check no others were hidden in the heather then said, "OK gone away." I slipped the lead over her head and we moved back to the centre of our line and waited for the others to move up. I felt exhilarated and relieved, whatever happened now, everyone knew she could do her job and I felt I could relax a bit.

Pen gave me a thumbs up and a little silent "Eek!" as she stepped up for her first turn. She needn't have worried Belle worked well for her too.

Watching Pen and the others work their dogs and taking my turns during the morning, the day took on a steady rhythm, as all around the moor seemed busy with life. Tiny clouds of insects hovered above the heather, from near and far came the call of Curlew and Lark. The Grouse jumped, playing their mating games, their familiar chuckle came to us both from a distance, carried on the wind, and close by as we steadily counted the birds in our designated area. A sense of peace and well-being overtook me in this wonderful place.

The first line of the count finished, we walked back to the cars and had a quick lunch, chunks of cake from Pen's tin and coffee from the flasks. The men ate copious quantities of sandwiches too, but I knew I would struggle to walk uphill if I ate too much, so stuck to a piece of cake. I gave Bird a rest and took Jeeves out after lunch. He did not play the fool as I had feared, instead worked with a joyful exuberance, throwing his heart and soul into the task. We finished our counting area for the day around three o'clock as planned, loaded weary, but satisfied dogs back into the trucks and made our steady way back to the farm.

Dinner was a success. "Better than your bangers, mash and beans, John." teased Graham.

"You don't have to eat it," said John. "Go hungry!"

They had been counting together for many years and the teasing was easy with the familiarity of long friendship. If Pen and I had worried about not fitting in, those qualms were soon laid to rest, all the guys made us feel very welcome. It was a relief for me to not have the undercurrent of a possible romance constantly present and I let my business worries slip into the back of my mind as the day's exertions took their toll and the heat of the fire wafted my anxious thoughts away.

We weren't late to bed, the early morning start, yomping over the moors all day and a good meal were fantastic aids to sleep. We initially moved from the kitchen to the sitting room with the intention of watching the News. Graham delighted everyone by falling asleep and snoring loudly, head lolling to one side, virtually the minute he sank into the deep sofa, so we all abandoned that idea and headed for bed.

20. A Careless accident.

On Monday, mist swirled thick as double cream around the farmhouse and it looked as though we may not get onto the moor to work the dogs. It is so easy to get lost up there or to lose a dog and essential to have good lines of sight for everyone's safety. Looking not just in the near distance, but out to middle and far distance helps to be aware of potential hazards in the terrain and to cover ground that looks likely habitat for birds.

Mike said "We'll wait a bit, this could lift, it often does by about nine o'clock."

We got books and newspapers, I wrote a couple of postcards, one for the girls in the practice, one for Mark. We had another look at the map and generally pretended to be relaxing, when in fact everyone's tell-tale glances to the window, gave away our fidgety desire to be up and away.

"Come on," said Mike eventually, "it looks a bit clearer let’s go up anyway and see how things are."

Today the moor was a very different place, its colours deadened by the mist as if we were seeing through cataracts. There was no perspective, just a silent opaqueness.

No matter, as predicted, the mist lifted silently, like the safety curtain on a stage, to reveal the rolling contours once more and it was game on!

The early morning mists lasted until Friday. Late starting, meant late finishing, so we had very little time to explore the local area, but I vowed that next time I came, I'd stay on a few days at the end and visit Jervaux Abbey, Leyburn and see more of the beautiful Dales. I'm not complaining, it was the most amazing week - we walked over stunning ground, wild and beautiful and became immersed in the sounds and smells of the moor. I was seduced by its wild beauty. Brett, would have captured the moor's essence in photographs effortlessly, captured moments, glimpses of this timeless place. His talent (one of the many) was to unerringly feel and capture atmosphere in his photography. I felt an ache as I thought of him. I thought of Mark too, I felt sure he would enjoy walking here and I had a little pang that he wouldn't experience this too.

Saturday, our last day on the moors dawned grey, wet and gusty. A steady mizzle fell in sheets blown by the wind like voile curtains in an open window. Clouds scudded across the sky and the grey light intensified the green tones of the grass. Brown heather glistened with moisture today, reflecting the light. Sphagnum moss sparkled, vivid as Peridot. Patches of silver lichen jewelled with tiny red spores nestled between the stout heather clumps and water pooled in boggy puddles that oozed with our footfall. Today's ground was deeper, the heather sprang and resisted each step. In patches, reedy ground sucked at our feet as we stepped high to cover the difficult tussocky terrain. Rain dripped off the brim of my hat onto my waterproof jacket and my face was damp with the humid air.

"No such thing as bad weather..." Said Pam ruefully.

"Only the wrong clothes." I chorused back.

Jeeves' coat was slick with rain and he couldn't have been less bothered, eyes bright, a slight steam rising off his back, he had loved working this morning and was up for more. Unfortunately for him we were on our way back to the trucks and we would be heading South the next day.

The accident happened so quickly. Almost back to the trucks, I caught the toe of my boot under a looped root of heather. The forward momentum of Jeeves on the lead in my left hand and my imprisoned foot made me fall awkwardly on a twisted knee. A sickening pop and an intense knife-like pain on the inside joint line made me cry out in pain, which immediately brought Pen and the guys around me.

"You OK Ellie?" Asked Pen her brown eyes dark with concern.

"No, I don't think so," I admitted, "Something has torn in my knee."

"Let me help you up," said Mike.

"No! Please don't move me for a minute." I could feel the blood draining out of my face and a tingling around my lips, the pain had made me feel light headed. Jeeves nudged me gently, "Alright boy," I said.

"Give me Jeeves," said Graham, "I'll load him into the car."

"Can you take Daisy too?" Said Pen handing her lead to him.

"I feel ridiculous," I said, trying to stave off the faintness with a deep breath. Cold came up from the ground through my coat and I shivered.

Graham came back with a thick and very hairy car rug which he draped round me. "Have a couple of these, it's paracetamol," he said.

I swallowed the pills and pressing down through my hands managed to ease my injured knee round. It was swelling rapidly and jabbed with a savage twang on the inside when I tried to straighten it.

"I think I may have torn a ligament or the cartilage," I said.

"Look, we'd better get you up off the floor and down to the surgery in Leyburn," said Mike.

Luckily, Graham and John had come up together in one vehicle today, so Graham was designated to drive my car. I managed to brace against my good knee and with a hand under each shoulder was hoisted into standing. Supported on each side, I slowly and painfully half hopped, half hobbled to the truck. By pushing the front seat back as far as it would go and with Pen supporting my leg, I slid painfully into the passenger seat.

"I thought the Physio was supposed to help the injured off the field, not the other way around!"

"I prefer it that way round," I replied honestly. The pain was now a steady pulsing ache with occasional excruciating stabs if I moved it at all. With the initial panic over, my brain crowded with worries; how would I get home and what would happen in the practice if I couldn't work? The drive off the moor along the rough tracks tested my fortitude.

The Doctor in Leyburn was a pleasant man in his late forties with prematurely grey hair. He made a competent job of looking at my knee (we Physio's can be a bit hard to please!) and explained that he had spent some time in Orthopaedics before deciding to move in to General Practice.

"I think that's a torn cartilage," he said, "the knee is properly locked about 20 degrees off fully straight and I can feel a click on the inside as I test it, so I think some cartilage is jammed in the mechanism." He gave me enough painkillers to fell an elephant, some crutches and said, "Your knee may need some surgery Ellie, but in the meantime probably at least 3 weeks off work for you and no driving till you feel safe to do an emergency stop."

All I could think about were my patients expecting me back on Monday, who could cover for me? and how would I manage if I couldn't work? My insurance wouldn't kick in until I'd been off for at least three months. This could push Touch over the edge financially. In the short term, how would I get me and the car home? I felt sick all over again, my optimism on arriving here had completely deserted me, I felt I was facing disaster.

Pen offered to take me and the dogs home with her the next day, but that meant leaving my car behind and quite a lot of our gear, plus it would be a real squash for the dogs. If we did that, when would I get back to get the car and how would I manage in the meantime?

During the last year I had worked so hard to launch the practice in its new premises and this was a massive blow. The injury couldn't have come at a worse time. Trying to build up enough work for two therapists, but managing alone for the moment, I was ready to look for a colleague but didn’t have one lined up yet, so I was stretched. Not to mention the massive jump in interest rates on my loan.

As if reading my mind, Pen said “I can see how worried you are Ellie, it’s just an idea, but could Mark help you out at all?”

“I don’t think so, why do you say that? What could he do?”

“I just thought he could talk over emergency strategies, it’s his job after all.”

“I think he’s away Pen and I’m not a client, he doesn’t know my business and I certainly can’t afford to employ him now.”

“You are one stubborn woman Ellie. You’re always helping other people but you never let anyone help you. Surely it can’t hurt to sound him out. He’s a friend, more than a friend if you ask me, he wouldn’t ask you to pay him.”

“No Pen, it’s not fair to load him with my troubles, he’s got his own business to run and enough troubles with losing Claire and trying to find a new girl online.”

“Oh don’t be stupid, he'll want to know. If you don’t phone him, I will!"

"No Pen don’t you dare.” Used to missing Brett when I felt worried or wanted to sound someone out, I realised that right now, it did feel comforting, Pen’s idea of talking it through with Mark. It was a new and strange sensation. “I dunno about ringing" I said, "He’ll think I'm being odd."

"No! My bet is he's dying to hear from you after a week away and men love a damsel in distress."

"He probably hasn't even registered I've been away."

"Yep and I'd bet my last Rolo you're wrong," said Pen "bet he's counting down the days until you're back."

I was surprised to find that Pen was quite right. I asked Mike if I could make a call. As I heard the rings, I imagined them echoing through an empty barn, with Mark probably still away, but he picked up on the third ring. He sounded genuinely delighted to hear my voice, which changed to concern for me, when I explained what had happened. It felt good to tell someone who understood. I was trying to make light of the whole getting home/leaving car dilemma when he cut in.

"Ellie, it's not a problem, if Mike or one of the others can collect me at the local station, I'll come up on the train and get you. I'll drive you and the dogs down on Monday in your truck."

"No, you can't do that," I said my cheeks flaming scarlet "You've got your own work and it will take hours to get up here."

"It'll be fine," he said his voice sounding like it was just a small favour, "I really don't mind, it's one of the perks of working freelance, I can be flexible. There's nothing in the diary that won't wait."

"Mark listen, I feel terrible, that's not why I rang."

"I know," he replied "but it ought to have been."

And that was that as far as he was concerned. Problem sorted.

“Really Mark, I’m sure I can manage, I don’t want you to miss work, you’re so busy.”

He totally ignored me and continued, "Give me Rose's address too,” he said, “I'll pop round and warn her. I'm sure she won't mind going in to do a bit of calling tomorrow to cancel Monday's appointments and then we can go from there."

“Mark, I can do all that from here, you mustn’t worry.”

“I sure you could, but you don’t need to because I’m here on the spot. What I think you should do is rest, and think about where you can get a replacement from at short notice. I know you don’t much like using agency staff but you may have to short term.”

“Mark...”

“Ellie, relax and let me help, OK?”

“OK, Mark, I give in, I can’t thank you enough.”

Pen just grinned when I told her and started humming "I drove all night" and "Radar love" 'til I was obliged to throw a cushion at her.

21. The journey home.

It is strange how different people behave when a group holiday ends, and they start to say goodbye. John, still in his field clothes and only heading a short way down the road was very matter of fact.

"Been a good week, girls. Your dogs did well. Get that knee right Ellie and hopefully we'll see you in the Summer. Thanks Mike - see you soon!" With a nod to us and a friendly handshake for Mike, he hopped into his truck and was gone in a scramble of gravel.

In his head, I felt he'd already gone on to whatever was next. I got the impression he lived very much in the here and now.

Graham on the other hand was lingering, chatting in a slightly nostalgic way, promising to forward photographs and already regretting the fun we'd had and the good cooking.

"Bye Ellie," he said giving me a bear hug "let me know what happens with your knee. Pen bring more of that amazing cake next time, I'm having withdrawal symptoms already. Safe journey home both of you, stay in touch."

Pen was fussing, about whether she had packed everything, but first and foremost about me.
"Sure you're going to be OK Hun? I feel bad leaving you... I can stay until Mark arrives if you'd like me to."
"Pen, it'll be fine," I said, knowing that when I waved her away it would indeed seem a bit strange. "See you in a couple of days."
"Don't forget to take your tablets either," she added as she turned to Mike.
"Mike, thank you for everything, it's been amazing, I've learned heaps and it's been great staying here. I've got lots of ideas from your renovation, for things I'd like to do at home. The builders are about to start on my upstairs bathroom and I may change my mind about decor. Angus is going to hate you! Look after Ellie, be firm, don't let her do anything mad, she can be stubborn as a mule."
Mike gave her a hug and said, "Between us, Mark and I will sort her out. You head off now, get home at a reasonable time."
We waved her off and Mike suggested we let the dogs have a romp in the field, so we set off for the gate, me limping on the crutches, Mike strolling beside me, setting his pace to mine in his instinctively courteous way. The dogs roared ahead but took care not to bump me. They had, without being told, set up a 'no-fly zone' around me as if they realised something was wrong.
Returning to the house when the dogs had had a good run around, it initially seemed rather quiet without the others, but Mike chatted in a comfortable way and we discussed some training ideas to work on with the dogs for the Summer over a cuppa. Drink finished, he glanced at his watch and said
"Shall we have a simple supper?"

"Sounds great to me," I replied.

"I'll pop into Leyburn for supplies now and then I'll be here when Mark rings to be picked up."

I started to say I was sorry to be such a nuisance, but he cut me short saying

"I'm just sorry you're injured, Ellie. Please don't worry, time is my own these days."

After he left, silence settled on the house, well except for the general traffic noise of the country, birds singing, chickens squabbling and an odd sheep calling to its lamb. Whilst Mike was gone, I settled down, leg up on a stool, ice pack in place over my football sized knee, to make some phone calls to my network of Physio friends. I needed to ask if they knew anyone who could cover for me whilst I was off. Call after call came up blank and I was beginning to think I would have to settle for an agency temp. On my last call, to a friend of a friend, which didn't seem very hopeful, I struck what I hoped was gold. There was a chance they could contact a friend of theirs. His name was Robin, and he was due to arrive in London the next day.

"He may well be looking for work, why don't you leave it with me to track him down. I'll get him to call you."

If this worked out it could be an amazing solution, I rang Rose to give her an update, trying to sound more upbeat than I felt.

"How are you, you poor thing?" She said.

"I'm cross with myself for being so clumsy and worried about the practice but hopefully it will all work out..."

"Please don't worry, you've had tons of good wishes from the patients, they all understand. I've cancelled your list for tomorrow already, so everything's in hand."

"You are such a star Rose, thank you for coming in on your day off."

"Not at all, Mark rang me and we hatched up an emergency plan. He's nice, isn't he?"

Clearly, she had joined the ranks of Mark's admirers, I was rapidly coming to the conclusion, that I had been holding out on a paragon that only I hadn't properly appreciated.

"He is very kind," I replied. "He's coming up to get me, which is above and beyond the call of duty. He has really got me out of a hole."

"He's been worried about you since you fell, but before that too. He called into the practice last week to ask about something. Excuse to ask if we'd heard from you, if you ask me. Good boyfriend material that one, take my advice snap him up before someone else does."

"Rose! Have you been talking to Pen? Mark is just a friend."

"Hmmm... We'll see."

Changing the subject before I felt anymore embarrassed, I said, "I may have found a New Zealand Physio called Robin to cover the patients until I can get back to work. I'll know definitely in the next couple of days. Keep your fingers and toes crossed Rose. If he does come, he can stay with me or we'll find him a room."

"Great! A locum would make life easier," she replied, and then rung off sending love and promising to pop in to see me when Mark and I got home the next day.

Feeling I'd made the best progress I could hope for with my calls, I removed the ice pack and did my ankle circling, toe pointing and pulling and bottom squeezes. I needed to encourage the circulation and use my leg muscles otherwise I'd be in trouble. Practice what you preach I thought ruefully!

As I exercised, I just hoped Robin would be able to help out at Touch.

Mike was soon back, laden with carrier bags containing everything for supper, and he'd also bought nibbles for Mark and me for the road down tomorrow. He was very thoughtful.

The morning had slipped away, lunchtime was upon us and I limped into the kitchen and balanced on one leg, with my crutches leaning against the work surface upside down. I always tell patients to rest them on the arm grips, not on the rubber stoppers at the bottom, to stop them falling over. I intended to help (but probably hindered) with the making of lunch.

Mark surprised us with his call to be collected from Northallerton station. He'd clearly left early and was a good hour ahead of anticipated arrival. Mike headed off again to collect him and I went back to the sofa to rest my knee, feeling frustrated and a bit useless.

Rose had taken me by surprise with her remarks and I felt nervous about seeing Mark now. Mark and I had become closer over the last year, we'd done a lot of things together because neither of us had a partner. Was this the start of something else?

We got on well, in a quiet comfortable way. We both spent time with Pen and Angus, but Dominic was often there too and I had never been sure if we might make a couple. We were both recovering from painful losses. I was a little afraid to take things any further, in case I lost him as a friend, but the truth was, I couldn't quite imagine life without him around now.

Hearing the truck pull up, I grabbed my crutches and stood up from the sofa, wincing as a stab of pain shot through my knee. I steadied myself until it had passed. Impatient with myself for being so slow, I hobbled to the front door. Mark's slim, tall form was just unfolding from the passenger side of the truck, his dark curly hair lifted back from his face by the breeze as he turned towards me. His face broke into a warm smile as he strode across the gravel drive and bent to give me a hug.

" Ellie, what a nightmare!"

As he folded his arms around me carefully, I noticed he smelled good of fresh, line-dried laundry and soap.

I was so pleased to see him and it was good, just for a moment, to lean against him and feel I had someone to rely on.

"Did you have a good journey?"

"It was fine, not a problem, I was more worried about you."

"It is so good of you to come."

"Don't be daft Ellie, you'd have helped me out, it’s what friends are for!"

The dogs were ecstatic to see him, so after a cup of tea, Mike proposed a walk to show him around. I regretfully declined and made myself busy packing up ready for the morning. I watched Bird and Jeeves bounding ahead of the two men towards the fields, tails wagging. When would I be back to doing my usual long walks, soon hopefully, otherwise I'd go nuts.

The evening passed very companionably and apart from a bad night's sleep, because it didn't seem there was any comfortable position for my knee and it kicked like a mule if I twisted it even slightly, I was ready to leave as planned after breakfast.

Mark narrowed his eyes slightly, "You OK?" he said as I presented my heavy eyes and pale face at breakfast, but kindly didn't press when I said "Fine." in reply.

Dogs walked and loaded, my gear stowed and the passenger seat pushed way back, I managed to sit down in my car and Mark lifted my leg in gently.

With much thanks, promises of updates and a plan to reconvene, hopefully fit, in the Summer, Mark and I took leave of Mike and headed for home.

I can honestly say it was a hideous journey. My leg did not take kindly to the movements of the car and the painkillers made me drowsy. Added to my bad night, during the first half of the drive, I drifted in and out of fitful sleep, pain prodding me awake like a malicious finger every so often.

"I like snoring." Mark said, as I apologised for being such a bad travelling companion. "It's the dribbling I hate!"

"Thanks a million, like I don't feel bad enough."

"Joking, joking," he replied putting his hands up in a gesture of submission. "I'm getting my own back, you gave me a hard time when I fell asleep on the way back from the wedding reception! Come on, we'll get a drink and a sandwich, you can take some more painkillers before we head off again."

Through the second part of the journey, Mark explained he'd spoken to Pen before breakfast this morning. They proposed that the dogs were dropped to her, which made sense. I'd intended to ask her if she would have them for me. They had also decided, because my little cottage had such steep stairs and no downstairs toilet, that I should take up residence in the ground floor guest room in Mark's barn. It seemed like my well-meaning friends had it all planned.

"I can't do that! You are so busy and I'd be in the way. I'm sure I can manage or can stay with Pen."

" Ellie it'll be fine, your cottage wasn't designed for someone hopping about on crutches, you'd break your neck. No-one is using that downstairs room and it has its own shower, no stairs to negotiate, it's much more practical. Pen has her two spare rooms stacked with tiles and bathroom stuff, they're about to rip the bathroom out."

I had been worried about managing the stairs at home, had forgotten about Pen's bathroom, and staying with Mark did solve a lot of problems, it was just very unexpected.

"Your Mum did say I could take you down to them to be looked after..."

"Oh no!" I said with feeling, "I need to be here for the practice." I wasn't sure I could cope with Mum taking me over.

"I thought that threat might make you more reasonable. Just say 'Yes Mark I'd like to stay'," he said glancing at my worried face.

After a moment's hesitation I said "Yes Mark."

"Well, I think I negotiated that one well! Pen said you'd be all kinds of difficult, being so bloody independent - her words not mine."

I gave him a push on his shoulder "You'll be wishing me gone, you don't know what you've let yourself in for!"

"No, I don't think I will," he said suddenly serious.

By the time we pulled up in front of Mark's barn after dropping the dogs with Pen, I was completely exhausted and long past any worries I may have had about staying with Mark. I hopped into the guest room, cleaned my teeth, swallowed a couple more painkillers and stretched out gratefully on the bed. Mark brought me a cup of tea and a small bell in case I needed him in the night. I declined any food and the next thing I knew it was morning and the tea was cold on the bedside table. I felt slightly disorientated as I woke, then as my knee jabbed with pain when I moved, everything came flooding back.

I gingerly lowered my leg to the floor, wincing as it protested, and stood up, pushing up on my two crutches in one hand and steadying myself on the bedside table with the other. I made it to the bathroom slowly and enjoyed a long shower, helping myself shamelessly to the shampoo and shower gel. The fluffy blue towel on the rail enveloped me in softness and once dry, I wrapped myself in the robe on the back of the door.

I heard a gentle tap at the bedroom door and Mark called "Can I come in?"

"Yes, come on in Mark."

"Morning sleepy head," he said laughingly, "You look better this morning. It's ten o'clock and Robin the Kiwi Physio has just rung the practice, I've got his number from Rose and he's expecting a call back whenever."

"Ten o'clock! I've overslept... Sorry Mark you should've woken me - do you need to get off to work?"

"Don't worry, I've got a meeting this afternoon, but have been working from here this morning. Do you fancy a brunchy type thing as you didn't eat last night?"

"I'm starving," I admitted, "but I can do it if you're busy."

"No, my piece de resistance is a full English. I'll bring your bag in first, you were asleep by the time I'd unloaded the car yesterday. Get dressed and hop on down to the kitchen."

"Ha Ha! Mocking the afflicted?"

"As if!"

"Oh, can I have Robin's number, and is it alright if I call him whilst you cook?"

"Yes, help yourself, his number is jotted on a note pad by the phone in the office."

I grabbed some loose-fitting track bottoms and a sweat shirt, easing the trouser leg over my foot at full stretch because there was no way the knee was bending very far. I made my way slowly to the office, cursing my bad leg.

I called Robin desperate to convince him to come and dig me out of a hole by covering the clinic. I was relieved to have someone so highly recommended, it's not easy to hand over your patients to someone else. We chatted for a while and he seemed too good to be true. I put a couple of clinical scenarios to him and he sounded very competent and not phased about handling a problem should one arise. He already had private practice experience. In London at the moment, Robin had planned to start his overseas trip with a few days holiday before job hunting, however, he agreed to come down the next day to settle in and start work on Thursday because of the emergency. I offered him my cottage until we could get any other accommodation sorted. He said he could certainly stay for a few weeks, if I needed him. I gave him directions to Touch from the station and put the phone down, before letting out a great "Whoop!" of relief.

"He's coming!" I shouted out to Mark "Woohoo."

"That's brilliant Ellie," said Mark appearing at the door in a calico apron. Crossing the room, he bent down to give me a hug, then, as he pulled away, our eyes met for a second and I thought he was going to kiss me. I'm sure he was, but he changed his mind and pulled away. He muttered something about the cooking, and turned away. Then turned back, without hesitating this time, took the two strides back and bent forward again, to kiss me on the mouth.

"Oh God, Ellie, I've wanted to do that for so long, now I've done it while you're incapacitated and here being looked after," he said, looking a bit rueful.

After a moment's hesitation, I replied by taking his face, which had softly, slowly, become so dear to me and returned his kiss, accepting gratefully the joy that came flooding through me. I suddenly felt fully alive again, after feeling for so long that part of me had died with Brett all those years ago.

"Ellie?" He said suddenly serious, his eyes scanning mine for reservations, "I know that this may seem sudden, too soon after Claire died, but, well, I knew Claire was dying for a long time before it happened and I think I did a lot of my grieving as I watched her in those last months. When you lost Brett, it was so sudden, the shock must have taken a long time to wear off before you could begin to grieve...It's just, I really want to be with you, this is not on the rebound for me and I couldn't bear to be second best for you. I want you to be sure you feel the same."

I looked back equally seriously, catching the hint of vulnerability behind his expression of resolve. "This is not second best for me," I said simply, "this is second time in love."

All the tension drained from his shoulders as I leaned in to hold him and feel his heartbeat slowing, the brush of his curly hair against my neck and to breathe in the warm, clean smell of his skin.

"Something's burning in the kitchen," I giggled pushing him away.

"Oh no! The eggs! I think your full English just became a half English."
"I don't care," I replied and I didn't, everything looked very good from where I was sitting, on cloud nine.

22. Something good happened.

We dawdled over Brunch, talking and holding hands across the table until Mark said reluctantly "Ellie, I have to be in Chelmsford at two o'clock, shall I drop you at the practice on the way? Then maybe either Rose or Jem can drop you back."

"Thank you, that would be great."

I hopped away to put my trainers on as Mark collected a couple of files and slotted them into his briefcase.

"Ready?" he called.

"Coming."

I balanced on my crutches outside the practice, kissed Mark goodbye and watched him pull away. I wondered where all this was going, but for now, I had a warm glow inside and a sense of contentment I hadn't felt for a long time.

Eagle-eyed Rose saw me outside and came to greet me, "Ellie, here you are, we've been so worried about you - how are you? "

"Apart from the dodgy knee, I'm fine" I replied.

"Come in off the street anyway, I'll put the kettle on and I can bring you up to speed."

Over a cup of tea, we ploughed through some normal post-holiday admin. and Rose updated me on what had been happening in the clinic. I wrote hand-over summaries for Robin in my current patient files, so he had essential information about each patient straight to hand. Every patient would be unfamiliar to him in the first few days, and he had busy lists booked. I hoped the summaries would help him settle in. I then rang several patients who had queries and realised as I glanced at the clock that three hours had slipped away.

Rose looked into my office and said, "Now Ellie, what about you? Are you going to book in with Robin for some treatment or are you seeing the Doc?"

"Actually Rose, I'm going to ring Walt, I'd love to think some Physio would sort this, but it probably needs surgery. I have pretty certainly torn a cartilage and the torn bit is caught inside the joint, blocking the mechanism of the knee. I maybe have some ligament damage too. The doctor up North said it needed surgery and I think he's right."

Walter Newton - Walt, was our local knee specialist. Second generation Orthopaedic surgeon, his Father had pioneered some of the early knee replacement surgery in the seventies. He was a really neat surgeon, who managed to operate with minimal trauma to the patient's soft tissues. More of an embroiderer than a carpenter. I picked up the phone and dialled his secretary Amanda.

"Hi Amanda, it's Ellie Rose from Touch Physiotherapy."

"Hi Ellie, what can I do for you?"

"I need an appointment for myself actually."

I explained my sorry tale to Amanda and asked when Walt could fit me in.

"Let me have a word with him Ellie, the clinics are busy this week, but I'm sure he'll fit you in somewhere."

"Thanks Amanda, do you have the practice number? I'm not staying at home at the moment and I can't remember my friend's number off-hand."

"Let me check...yes I have it, I'll get back to you."

I wasn't expecting a reply that day, but before Rose dropped me home, the Practice phone rang and she passed it to me "It's Walt Newman for you Ellie."

"Hello Walt, it's good of you to call me back so quickly."

"Hi Ellie, Amanda says you're in a bit of bother."

"Completely hobbled."

"Can someone get you here early tomorrow? If you get here about eight thirty, I can see you before clinic starts."

"Are you sure?"

"Yes, yes no problem, who's going to fix my patients if you're out of action."

I laughed "Well if you put it like that... thank you, I am sure I can be there."

"See you tomorrow Ellie."

I put down the phone and turned to Rose.

"What time is Robin arriving tomorrow?

"He said about two o'clock."

"I have an early appointment with Walt but should be back in time to show him round here and my house. Walt offered to see me tomorrow before clinics."

"Oh, that's good Ellie, can you get there? Jem could probably take you if you need a lift. I could, but I think I'd better be here to sort things for Robin and organise his list."

"I'll see if Pen or Mark can do it, but may take you up on that offer of a lift with Jem otherwise. What a mess Rose. This injury was incredibly bad timing, we were keeping our heads above water against the economic odds and working so hard, now this has happened!"

"Come on," she said giving me a brief hug round the shoulder "It's no good fretting Ellie, we can't change anything. We'll work it out and something good will come of it, nothing is all bad."

I thought back to this morning and smiled to myself, something good had already happened.

Rose and I called it a day about five and I asked her if she would drop me at Pen's, I was desperate to see the dogs.

Pen's house was a hive of activity. The builders had clearly started on the work upstairs and the large parking area at front of the house was a litter of vans and equipment. I saw Pen moving about the kitchen and limped over to the kitchen door on my crutches avoiding all the trip hazards.

"Hiya."

"Hi Ellie, come on in, sit yourself down, how are you today?"

"I'm not bad, hope you don't mind me arriving unannounced, Rose dropped me, I wondered how Jeeves and Birdie are?"

"Course not, don't be daft. The dogs're fine, I've just fed the ravening hounds, I'll go and get them if you like, just a mo."

I watched her stride off through the back door and across the lawn, towards the kennels, curly hair bouncing. She disappeared from view for a second but I heard the familiar hubbub as the dogs saw her approach. Very shortly, my two dogs appeared round the side of the house at a gallop.

"Birdie! Jeeves!" As I called, they pulled up short, ears cocked and then bundled into the kitchen towards the sound of my voice.

"Hey guys, I've missed you" I said as they crowded round, ears back, tails wagging, weaving round me for strokes and ear scratches. It was good to see them.

"They've been in the kennels for a bit this afternoon. Mine have too, the builders have been coming and going, leaving doors open, so I think they're safer in there. I don't want them getting out. They can come in again as soon as the builders have gone."

"They don't look too hard done by."

"So, how's it going?"

"Yes, I'm getting there, Robin, the New Zealand Physio, arrives tomorrow on his white charger. Rose has transferred all my appointment lists over- he's in for a busy few weeks, I can tell you. Then Walt Newman the Knee surgeon has given me an appointment for tomorrow morning before clinics, to get my knee checked. Robin's having my cottage for the time being, Rose has already been in and changed the bed and put some stuff in the fridge for him and I'm staying at Mark's until I know what's happening with my knee, so it's all organised. Everyone has been great, including you."

"Rose will be loving it, bet she's in her element coping with a crisis. What about the Barn, you and Mark getting on OK?"

"Good, good." I said feeling a blush spreading up my neck.

"Ha! You're blushing! Tell all immediately! Just let me get some tea."

"Um well, I don't know, things took a bit of an unexpected turn this morning." I said as Pen plonked down a steaming mug beside me. "Not quite sure what happened, but Mark was cooking breakfast and came over to give me a hug when I'd heard Robin could do the locum cover for me and then we caught each other's eye and the hug became a kiss and it felt great ..."

"Well Hallelujah! You two have been driving Angus, Dom and me nuts, so good together, but not getting on with it."

"Pen, I have thought about him a lot, but I wasn't sure he felt the same. It has just been great to have such a good friend, I didn't want to muck that up. I think I only realised things had changed, when I was stranded up in Yorkshire."

"Well I know he's thought about it as well. Dom asked me if I knew whether you might be interested, because Mark's been agonising and not wanting to get hurt and not wanting to upset you."

"Has everyone been taking bets?"

"I think everyone except you has been watching with baited breath. Ask Rose, she said to me she thought you'd make a good couple."

"You lot are impossible."

"Talk of the devil, that's Mark's car just pulled in isn't it?"

Pen waved through the window and beckoned him in. Mark appeared at the kitchen door his tall lean body blocking the light momentarily, as he fought his way through the dogs and bent to kiss me keeping it to a chaste brush on the cheek. His familiar clean smell enveloped me for an instant and set my heart racing.

"Unhand my wounded friend you cad!" Said Pen, mock attacking him with a tea towel.

"I don't think so," he laughed ducking out of the way, "The lady is mine!"

Jeeves tried to grab the tea towel that Pen was flapping, Bird danced round barking and mayhem ensued for a minute.

"Well when you two have finished, the "lady" needs to beg a lift tomorrow. Walt has said he can see me tomorrow, but I need to be in Chelmsford by half eight, could either of you take me? Otherwise Rose has volunteered Jem."

"No don't bother Jem." Mark said "I can run you there."

"Are you sure? Please don't cancel work."

"He'll have *his* white charger at the door." teased Pen, still fending off Jeeves. "All these men falling at your feet Ellie..."

"No! I won't have a word said against Mark," I laughed, "he's the roof over my head after all."

"Oh! Be careful," said Mark, "Or you may be walking there tomorrow Ellie Rose. Well, hobbling I should say...Anyway, I'm clearly outnumbered here, where's Angus to defend me when I need him?"

"I'm sure you can defend yourself." Said Pen "Take this girl home, she looks shattered and I'm sure that leg should be up with an ice pack on it after an afternoon at work."

I gave the dogs a last cuddle and left them looking at me with big sad eyes through the door. I really missed them.

Morning came after another bad night. I was worried about my knee, a million hand over instructions for Robin kept whirring in my brain and I was thinking about Mark. It felt good when I was with him, I felt ready to move on. Then when I was alone, I felt sad as Brett slipped away from me a little more. He would only slip into a corner of my heart somewhere, he would always be with me, I knew that really, but his memory had been my constant companion for so long, it felt strange to be letting him go.

I eased my leg painfully out of bed and showered, then put on some shorts under track bottoms ready for my appointment. Mark was moving about in the kitchen already and I hobbled out to swallow a cup of coffee. I didn't think I could manage food, I felt very apprehensive. If the knee problem was anything too complicated and I couldn't work for a while, I wasn't sure what would happen to the clinic.

"Hey Ellie," said Mark coming across the kitchen to give me a kiss, "you look peaky, have you had another bad night?"

"Yeah not brill, I couldn't stop my mind whirring."

"Well I'm not surprised, hopefully things will be clearer when you've seen Walt and met Robin today. It's been a mad few days."

"It's not just that Mark, I need to talk to you about something. Do you? I mean, does it, ever feel like you're being disloyal to Claire when we're together?"

He paused for a moment a small cloud crossing his eyes. "Ellie, up til now, everything has felt wrong, moments when I felt happy made me guilty, planning the new business made me feel like I was leaving her behind. Those awful dating agency meetings, I felt like a traitor. It feels different with you, we've got to know each other gradually and I know Claire would like you, she was lovely, she would want me to be happy too."

"Everyone says the same to me and I know they're right. I feel good when I'm with you, not guilty but I've never wanted to be with anyone except him, not since he died so this is strange."

"Perhaps we both have to get used to being happy again, it's not like this takes away from what we had with Brett and Claire or from the pain of losing them. I'd like to think we're a credit to them."

I nodded thoughtfully, I liked that idea.

You haven't had anything for breakfast yet. Would you like a coffee? There is some in the cafetière, and what would you like to eat?

"Not really hungry," I said perching on a high stool, "can I just grab a banana?"
"Sure." said Mark pushing the fruit bowl towards me. "We should probably get going soon, in case we catch the rush hour traffic."
We had a good run to the small private hospital on the outskirts of Chelmsford, parked up and I made my painful way to the outpatient clinics. Amanda was already at her desk and hailed me.
"Ellie, hi! Oooh, that looks painful, you poor thing. I'll buzz Walt and let him know you're here."
"Thanks Amanda."
I sat next to Mark in the waiting area and he gave my hand a reassuring squeeze.
Walt appeared from one of the consulting rooms, strode across the waiting area, full of radiant energy as ever, beamed at us both and said "come on in Ellie, what have you been up to?"
I followed him into the consulting room on my crutches, lowered myself awkwardly into the chair on my good leg sliding my painful leg forward and retold my story to Walt. Despite his jovial manner I knew he was watching me walk and move and was already assessing (as all good clinicians do). When he had taken the history, I transferred onto the examination couch in the corner and he checked out the swelling, felt the movement, noting that I couldn't straighten at all, even when he assisted, and then put me through the same series of ligament and cartilage tests as the GP up in Yorkshire.
"It's not great is it?" I said feeling anxious about the serious look on his face.

"You're going to need some surgery," he said, "I can see you in my NHS Clinic, but there will be a wait, have you got any private medical insurance?"

"I have," I replied, "When I started working for myself, Dad insisted I took it out. It's a bit of a nightmare for me being off work for too long. I need to check if it covers this."

"In that case, why don't you speak to them? I will too, I'd like to do one of the new keyhole surgery procedures if they agree. Hopefully we can remove whatever is blocking the knee, probably a tag of meniscus and tidy up in there. Your recovery will be much quicker than the old open-knee procedures. I'll look at your Cruciate ligaments whilst I'm in there but they don't seem to be damaged."

I could tell he was excited, he was one of the pioneers of arthroscopic surgery and it was amazing how much could be done through three tiny holes and how quickly patients recovered. I on the other hand felt less enthusiastic about any kind of operation.

"If I get the OK from my insurance, when could you fit me in?"

"We'll speak to Amanda, but I think beginning of next week. Let's get you on your feet ASAP."

Walt shook my hand, joking that I would probably be a nightmare patient and left me with Amanda, giving a cheery wave.

"Next Tuesday?" She said, "you'd need to arrive at seven thirty and probably plan for a one-night stay."

"Yes, the sooner the better. I just need to confirm with my insurers."

"That's fine," she replied, "contact me with any problems. We'll send out all your pre-op instructions in the post, although I know you know it all already."

"No, I'd like that," I admitted, "it feels weird being on this side of the equation. Could they be sent to the practice please, I can't manage the stairs at home, they are more of a ladder than stairs, so I'm staying with a friend."

"Sure," she replied, handing me an appointment card, "see you next week Ellie, it'll be strange you being the patient!"

Too right!

Putting the card in my back pack I set off towards Mark and told him the news.

"Well that's good, I think. Sort of what you were expecting?"

"Yup, I need to get it sorted, I will be going stir crazy soon."

Mark laughed, "Does that mean cranky and miserable? Should I turn you out now?"

"I won't be showing you all my worst character traits yet," I replied, "Something for you to look forward to."

He gave me a quizzical look...then said, "You good to go?"

"Yes, I haven't got anything else to do here, if you could drop me at the practice I can be there to meet Robin."

23. A Kiwi locum.

Robin arrived promptly at two o'clock with a huge rucksack, bulging at the seams, on his back and a slightly jet lagged appearance. Handsome in a 'boy-next-door' kind of way, his mid brown hair was short cropped and the crinkles around his eyes suggested a ready smile.

"You must be Ellie." The suspected smile flashed like sunshine on a winter day. "The crutches are a bit of a giveaway."

"Robin, hi, I'm so pleased you're here, I'm sorry you've been dragged in like this, your feet can't have touched the ground!"

"No worries, I'm not quite into my UK sleep pattern yet, but I'll be fine in a couple of days."

I turned towards the desk where Rose was sitting. "Let me introduce you to Rose, she and Jen are your admin. Team. hey know the practice inside out and will get you through all the workings of the place."

"Pleased to meet you Rose." he said, extending a hand and smiling warmly.

Evidently won over by a pretty face, I was surprised to see a hot blush creeping into her cheeks as Rose said "Hello Robin, we are really pleased to see you. Can I get you a drink? Tea? Coffee?"

"I'd love a cup of tea, strong, with milk and no sugar please."

She bustled away to the kitchen, making a mime of fanning herself behind his back and mouthing "he's gorgeous," to me.

"You're going to be busy from tomorrow," I said trying not to smile at Rose. "I hope I've left legible summaries in the files for everyone and if you can't understand my scrawl, you can always ring me. Rose has the number where I'm staying. I'll pop in from time to time and after the op on Tuesday and I'll be needing some treatment myself."

"Look you're not to worry; Rose and I have it covered, haven't we Rose?" He said as she returned with his cup of tea and two chocolate biscuits.

Robin wasn't being over-confident or pushy, on the contrary, he just seemed kind and calmly confident. I was feeling better already. If the receptionists don't like you, you are done for, there are many subtle ways they can make your life hell. It was more than a load off my mind that Rose seemed won over already. If she gave Robin the thumbs up to the patients, it would smooth his way.

"Shall I show you round?"

"Great."

I was very proud to walk him around the new clinic - it was a lovely place to work and I was pleased when he said "Wow Ellie, you've got a really lovely space here, it's got a nice feel."

"I love it but I’m biased. I do appreciate you coming at such short notice, so I hope you'll be happy."

Word travels fast, by the time we'd done the tour, I'd shown him how the machines work and where all the supplies were stored, Jem popped by to meet him. He offered to take us to my cottage so Robin could settle in. Curiosity had got the better of him I suspect and I did just wonder if he wanted to check out this new boy that Rose was so taken with.

Before we left, Robin rummaged in his rucksack and produced a document folder which he held out, "my certificates and ID."

Rose said she would take them to be photocopied and return them in the morning.

Following Robin and Jem to the car on my crutches, I noticed how he inclined his head towards Jem, his whole body saying "I'm listening." Jem can be shy, but he had effortlessly drawn him out. As I got to know him better, I realised he had this quality, people felt comfortable with him and he inspired confidence and confidences.

Warm for Spring, a lovely sunny day meant Robin saw the new part of town at its best as we drove through. The red brick houses seemed mellow in the sunshine. Most of them were newly built, so the gardens were still raw, but it was easy to see that people cared. In time the newness would soften to something prettier. My cottage was further out, where the original village had been and here there was less uniformity. The houses varied in size, shape and age. Some were half clad with ship-lap, a nod to the Dutch influence in Essex. Mature fruit trees scattered petals like confetti and the gardens were full of Spring colour. Currently decked in white lace flowers, like spring brides, the hawthorn trees that lined the paths nodded graciously in the wind. As we arrived near the cottage, Robin could see that roads and houses gave way to fields at the edge of the town.

Jem turned his newly acquired pride and joy, a Vauxhall Astra, onto my tiny drive and pulled to a halt. It was still a struggle to get in and out of most cars, so I eased out of the front seat gingerly and adjusted my balance before walking to the front door. As I opened the door, post pushed back in a fan shaped sweep and fresh air disturbed the sleepy stillness of the room.

"Come in, come in, make yourself at home. I can show you down here, but you'll have to negotiate the stairs yourself to see the bedroom."

I picked up the post and leaflets cluttered behind the door, dipping in balletic fashion by bending my trunk forward on my good leg, with the injured one out behind as a counterbalance. I added the letters to the pile made by Rose when she had been in to make the place tidy for Robin. Nothing very interesting looking I noted.

Robin dropped his rucksack beside the sofa and said "Are you sure you're happy to hand over your cottage Ellie?"

"Yes, of course, I can't be here at the moment, so make use of it. I'm staying with a friend, Mark. He has a downstairs guest room which makes life easy, I could do ordinary stairs but my 'ladder' stairs are a bit risky! Mark asked if you'd like to eat with us tonight?"

"Oh look, thanks, that's really thoughtful, but I'm going to crash early if you don't mind, so I'm fit for work tomorrow."

Jem said, "Rose didn't know what you like, but she's stocked the fridge with basics to get you started and I've brought some lasagne and salad from home if you'd like it tonight.

"Brilliant, that's so kind of you and Rose, thanks. Ellie I may never go away again, I'm not used to being so spoilt."

"Lulling you into a false sense of security." I laughed, "Rose is a shocking tyrant at work - you'll see!"

I went through all I could think of about the house, gave Robin my spare key and finally left him to it. Jem said he'd drop me back to the barn, for which I was very grateful, my leg was aching and the knee felt swollen inside my trousers.

As we pulled away from the cottage, I suddenly thought, "I should have told him about the back door." The handle looks like it would open from the outside, but in fact it's a deadlock, so you have to have the keys with you or you get locked out. I mentioned it to Jem who said, "Shall we go back?"

"No, it's alright, I'll ring when I get to the Barn, I doubt he'll be doing any gardening today," I joked.

Jem said he would get Rose to warn him the next day, if I didn't remember to ring and we continued on our way. As it happened, I fell asleep when I got in and completely forgot to ring that evening. This led to an embarrassing incident...

The next morning, I had a phone call from Rose, "No need to worry Ellie."

"Worry? What's happened?" My stomach did a somersault.

"I've rescued Robin from Mrs Mallory's house and he's made it to work on time. He's seeing patients now."

Mrs Mallory was my lovely neighbour at the cottage, she was on the shady side of fifty, loved country and western music and ran a sandwich delivery business from home.

"What on earth happened?" I asked aghast.

Choking back the giggles Rose said "Robin had a shower this morning, wrapped himself in a towel and then took his tea out into the garden. The wind caught the back door and he was locked out."

"Oh no, the deadlock." I groaned.

"He had to walk round to Mrs Mallory just in his towel... She was in the kitchen with her sandwich makers. Fortunately, she phoned me to come and rescue him, but they were in no hurry to be rid of him. They thought all their Christmases had come at once when he walked in. By the time I arrived, he was drinking tea and eating an egg sandwich looking like one of the Chippendale's. Fortunately, he isn't the shy and retiring type."

I had to laugh, Mrs Mallory's sandwich team are her friends from line dancing club and they are a jolly and occasionally raucous bunch, who would be dining out on this for weeks.

"Gosh what an introduction to the town, that was my fault, tell him I am so sorry Rose."

"It brightened up my morning too." She replied.

I think Rose had a small crush on my locum.

24. The operation.

Dom and Vale came down from London for the weekend on Friday, we were all tired, so elected to go to the Prince of Wales to eat rather than shop or cook. We edged our way through the crowded pub and found one of the scrubbed wooden tables with mismatched chairs that was free and ordered from the selection of real ales at the bar. We all decided to indulge in the homemade chicken pie which came to the table golden and glorious, oozing creamy sauce as we cut into the pastry crust. The toast from Dom was, "Mark and Ellie, thank goodness we can stop holding our breath!"

"I'll drink to that," said Vale.

I laughed as we chinked glasses, "You guys need more in your lives..."

"Talking of which," said Dom "what are the plans for this weekend?"

Clearly anything too athletic was out for me, so unless they could persuade Pen or Angus, tennis would be difficult. At the moment I could just about umpire, even ball-girl would be too much. We decided on a trip to the pictures for tomorrow evening and settled on the new Robin Hood with

Kevin Costner despite a desperately made bid for Terminator 2 by Dom.

"I thought you'd like it, pick up some tips for your op next week," he said to me.

"Very funny Dom, hopefully it won't be that complicated. Mind you," I said, pushing my empty plate away, and patting my sides, "if that was the condemned woman's last meal, I shall die happy, I'm so full up."

"Leave Ellie alone," said Vale "she needs cheering up and happy endings, not blood and guts. You boys can go to Terminator and Ellie and I will see Robin Hood."

"Indeed not!" said Dom, "However doubtful your taste Ladies, we shall gallantly escort you, shan't we Mark?"

"Well I can hardly say no now, can I?"

As Saturday was a fairly dreary, wet day we mainly lazed about, reading the papers and chatting. Even the dogs didn't seem very keen to be out when Mark and I went to the farm to give them a run. Well, truthfully, Mark ran them, I walked a little way and watched. I was itching to be able to walk properly again, but at the same time felt absurdly nervous about the operation on Tuesday. I got butterflies every time I thought about it. To know so much about what can go wrong, isn't always a good thing! Pushing operation nerves firmly to the back of my mind, I focused on watching the dogs and spent some time visualising everything going incredibly well instead.

As a thank you for all they were doing for me, I decided to do something for Pen and Mark, so asked the others if they fancied a roast on Sunday. I invited Pen and Angus, Dom and Vale, and got Mark to drive me to Joe, the Butcher in town, before we needed to get ready to go out.

"What have you got for a special roast, Joe?"

"I go for the rib of beef Ellie" he held it up, "look at that, lovely."

I stashed it in the fridge and decided as I was getting ready to go out, that tomorrow, I'd go the whole nine yards with Yorkshire pudding, crispy, roast potatoes, lots of fresh veggies and horseradish gravy.

Even the boys had to admit that Robin Hood was fun.

"Alan Rickman was brilliant as the Sheriff of Nottingham," Mark said as we left the cinema.

"He's already a favourite of mine from *Truly, Madly, Deeply."* I'd seen it the year before and loved it.

Vale hadn't seen it, so I promised to lend her the video. It was a poignant story for me and I'd identified with the main character's disorientation when her boyfriend died. In the early days after Brett died, I liked to think he was still with me and carried on talking to him as if he was, like Juliet Stevenson in the film. The story was also full of hope and looking at Mark, feeling his arm casually round my shoulders, I felt that perhaps, I had finally done with grieving.

Despite having to hobble around the kitchen, I managed a decent roast beef the next day, with Mark's help and my trusty perching stool.

"Food always tastes better when you haven't cooked it yourself," Pen said, closing her knife and fork together after devouring seconds of Yorkshire pudding and gravy."

"Thank you, Ellie, it was delicious." Said Angus raising his glass of red wine, "Compliments to the chef."

"Chef's," I said "Mark helped as well, I can't take all the credit."

"Yep," said Vale, "he's a keeper, very handy in the kitchen."

“Alessandra always got us in the kitchen, do you remember Mark?” said Dom, ”It was fun, she’s great your Mum.”

“She can’t abide useless men who need to be looked after all the time,” said Mark.

“I love her already,” said Vale, “God bless Mom’s with attitude.”

“She’s got that alright,” Mark laughed.

As Sunday afternoon drew to a close, Dom and Vale collected their weekend bags and said goodbye, both gave me big hugs and promised to be in touch through Mark, to see how I was. Pen and Angus also made a move and Pen promised to be back on Tuesday bright and early as she was dropping me off at the hospital.

Mark and I cleared the kitchen and after a cuddle and a long kiss, we reluctantly separated. As I lay in my bed looking up at the ceiling I wondered when the moment would be right to sleep together for the first time. All through my grieving, sex had not been on my mind at all and the thought of making love with anyone but Brett seemed impossible, but suddenly the desire to be with Mark was intruding on more of my waking thoughts than I’d care to admit and I tossed and turned fretfully.

Monday dragged and I moved restlessly around the barn, not settling to anything, as the clock ticked its countdown. I slept badly on Monday night too and as Tuesday dawned, I was relieved to be going in for my op to get it out of the way. Mark gave me a hug and said “See you this evening, be thinking about you today,” as he headed off to work.

It was a glorious bright morning, still a little crisp but with more than a hint of Summer to come in the air. Pen and I took the back roads to avoid the worst of the traffic through Chelmsford and arrived at the hospital as planned at seven thirty. Pen dropped me outside the reception area, parking was terrible and I assured her that I'd be fine, not to waste time trying to park. I walked in and announced myself at reception. I felt a curious mixture of being at home in the hospital environment; the antiseptic smell, ringing phones, hushed chatter and bleeps were all familiar from my years before Touch. But also, I felt as apprehensive as every other patient checking in for surgery.

A cheerful, dark haired, young nurse came to collect me and showed me to my room. It was tastefully, but blandly decorated in the style of a middle-budget hotel chain room. On the bed lay the dreaded open-back theatre gown.

"Settle in and make yourself comfy," she said, "no need to gown up yet, we'll come in and do some pre-op checks and the Anaesthetist will come in for a chat first."

"Thanks." I settled in the arm chair and flicked through the TV channels, unwittingly catching a nature documentary, just at the moment when a buffalo calf was being brought down by lions. The graphic image, upset me and I switched off, opting for my book, but I couldn't clear the image from my head. Distraction came in the form of the Anaesthetist.

"Ellie, hi, won't be long before you go down now. Are you comfortable to come down to theatre awake, or would you like a pre-med to make you drowsy?"

"No, I'm fine without."

"You'll probably come round more quickly and with less sickness," he explained. He then had me sign off the usual consent forms and drew a large black arrow on my leg, indicating without a doubt which one was for surgery.

The nurse came back to get me into my gown and on the bed for my last checks and to wash the leg with a pink antiseptic. The Physio came next, recognised me and said

“Well I don’t need to teach you how to do the exercises or use crutches.” Then Walt popped his head in and said “See you down there Ellie.”

As the porter, checked my name off on his clip board, clicked off the brakes and wheeled the bed down to theatre, a sense of detachment came over me with a curious feeling of inevitability. I wasn’t sure I liked being out of control, on a conveyor belt like this it reminded me of how I felt after Brett died, but I could stop clutching to control everything now. That nightmare was over and Mark was teaching me to feel safe again.

The anaesthetist was waiting in his green surgical scrubs to put a line in the back of my hand. “Just a scratch now,” he said, as he slid the needle into the vein and taped it in place. He carried on chatting about this and that as he prepared the anaesthetic and then asked me to count back from ten.

We all think we’ll be able to resist falling asleep, but I doubt I made seven, before I knew nothing more until I was waking up in recovery.

Shadowy faces floated above me and I was aware of pain in my knee, it felt huge, I later realized, because of the thick compression bandage around it.

“I need a pillow under my knee” I called out fretfully to the nurses. It seemed forever until one came to help. I also felt very confused, “I should be meeting my boyfriend Mark” I said to someone.

“All part of the recovery process, you’re fine, try to relax.” They reassured me, and I must have been given some pain meds, because the next thing I remember, was waking in my room and noticing it was mid-afternoon.

“Hello sleepy head,” said the dark-haired nurse, “We thought you were never going to wake up.”

She left some tea and toast on the side, of which I managed a few mouthfuls, but it tasted peculiar, metallic and I didn't want it.

Walt came in, "Hi Ellie, the operation was a bit more complicated than we thought. I've removed a tag of cartilage but also a small fragment of bone, which must've come away as the ligament was wrenched when you fell. I've also had to do some shaving and other tidying up inside as well. Your knee looked a bit older than you do, once I got inside."

"It's really painful, more than I expected. Is everything alright?"

"Yes, everything is fine, it's more painful because of all I had to do. Try to have enough pain relief so that you can do your exercises and get some sleep."

"I'm not great at taking meds."

"Yes, but it will help you recover more quickly, I'd rather you took them for the first few days. I think you'll be fine to go home tomorrow, providing you can manage the stairs with your crutches. Because I did more than expected Ellie, I'd like you to have the compression bandage on to start with and so movement will be restricted at first, everything is very raw in there."

All that afternoon, I drifted in and out of sleep. I managed to stay awake, just about, when Mark came in about six. He looked smart-dishevelled, straight from work, jacket over his shoulder, tie loosened and his white shirt creased, but he looked good to me. His concerned frown eased as I greeted him and he smiled in return. Hospitals did not hold happy memories for him because of Claire, he'd said how much he hated them and I realised that being here to support me must be difficult.

He bent over to kiss me. "How are you feeling?"

"Honestly? A bit beaten up," I replied and explained about the operation being more complicated.

"Sounds horrible, no wonder you aren't feeling on top of the world. It's a relief to see you safe and sound," he continued in a rush, "I know I'm being stupid, but I've been worried all day Ellie, I kept thinking something terrible could happen and I couldn't bear to lose you as well."

"Hey, don't think like that, I'm not going anywhere, I promise. I'm sure I'll feel better tomorrow, Walt says I can still come home providing I manage the stairs."

"Just seeing you there in that bed looking so pale.."

"Shhh, don't, it must be horrible for you being back after what happened to Claire, but I am going to be fine."

I was still drowsy, so Mark passed on love sent from everyone and left when my dinner arrived on a tray. I didn't mind, I suspected that just the smell of a hospital was enough to trigger bad memories for him. I loved him even more for being there for me despite all that, it said a lot about him. He'd taken the next day off and said he'd come to get me as soon as I was ready.

Initially, I'd protested, but in the end, I really wanted him with me and I felt safe being able to relax and let him nurture me after all the years of feeling I had to cope alone.

The next morning a young Physio student was sent to teach me how to walk on crutches and do the stairs. A little joke on the part of the other Physios I suspected. She did a great job of explaining it all to me and was duly admiring of how quickly I'd picked it all up! She clearly began to smell a rat however when I was so slick with my first flight of stairs and asked if I'd had an operation before. I was able straight faced to say no. I omitted to tell her the hundreds of times I'd demonstrated crutch walking though. She poked her head back round the door of my room later that morning, grinning, pointed at me with her eyes narrowed and said, “Very funny!” Someone had let the cat out of the bag.

I had all my instructions and tablets by lunchtime, so Mark came to pick me up. There was an awkward moment in the car when the residual anaesthetic and the bends in the country lanes made me feel very queasy. Fortunately, we were close to a pub car park and a few moments of fresh air sorted me out. Seeing me feeling so sick, made Mark anxious again. Between reassuring him this was normal and feeling rotten, I was glad to see the barn and collapse onto the couch with my leg up. My bedroom was full of flowers from Dom and Vale, Rose and Robin at the Clinic, Mark and Mum and Dad. Pen had sent up a casserole for our dinner tonight and a huge cake. The cake tin had a note attached - *be up to see you tomorrow, be good!*

People are so kind, I was touched by how much everyone was spoiling me and how thoughtful they had been. It was nice to feel loved.

The first two weeks after the operation were taken up by how slow I was at everything and surprisingly, how tired and washed out I felt. However, now I was feeling better and better so my compression bandage and crutches were beginning to irk me. I longed to be out across the fields again with my dogs. I wanted to be back in the Clinic again too. Robin was doing an amazing job, he had stepped in without missing a beat. Rose was a slave at his feet and most of the patients had transferred to him with a good grace after their initial worries about him not being me. I heard nothing but good reports.

It's a rare phenomenon, Locums are often not embraced readily, patients tend to mistrust change. So much so, that usually, when I went away from the Clinic for short breaks, I had ceased to employ one. I had growing respect for Robin's people skills and let's face it charm.

One evening, Mark said, "Why don't you offer him a permanent job? Before you hurt your knee, you were almost ready to look for a Physio to come and work with you at Touch."

"He's exactly the sort of person I was thinking of, but I don't think he'd be interested, he came over to travel in Europe."

"You don't know 'til you ask, offer him flexible hours and let him have a long weekend each week to travel or long holidays. He's a good Physio and fits in well, don't let him slip through your fingers."

"I'm not sure if I can afford him permanently though," I replied picking at a rough quick on my thumb.

"Well, I have an idea," said Mark, "Simple solution, you move in here with me and let him rent your cottage. You reduce your overheads, he gets great accommodation and a flexible job to fund his travels. I get your warm and lovely self to come home to. If it doesn't work out, nothing lost, you go back to your cottage and find another Physio when the time is right."

I looked up startled, his voice sounded light and casual as if he'd offered me a cup of tea or a lift into town and I couldn't believe what he had just said. The concern in his eyes as he studied my reaction, belied the lightness in his voice.

"But..." I started to say, a hundred small worries flitting across my mind.

"But what? We'll soon know if it doesn't work out and you aren't burning any bridges. We’ve been the easiest and best of friends for over a year now haven’t we?"

I opened my mouth to speak but he ploughed on. "After what happened to Claire, I thought I would never feel the same about anyone ever again, and I don't, you're not her. I wouldn't want you to be. I'm not Brett either. You're you and I've been so happy to have you here with me."

"Look this is...well, I don't know...I mean... I am going to have to think about this."

"No Ellie you don't! Stop over-thinking and go with your instincts. Does this feel right? Good even?"

"Yes! It absolutely does, but I think you've gone a bit mad, I think everyone will think we're mad too. We haven't been officially going out together, except as friends, until now, and suddenly I'm moving in..."

"Well, when it works brilliantly, they will have to think again."

He leaned across, took my hands and held my gaze steadily, "Ellie Rose, if I am very careful not to break you, and we do something creative with your leg, can we make love, now, tonight?"

Returning his gaze with a slow smile, I said "Mark Roxbury, I thought you would never ask."

The carefully constructed defences I'd been living behind for five years, which kept me safe, whilst I nursed my wounds, yet isolated me from the vibrant pulse of fully living, had been breached quietly and gently without my even realising. I stood poised at the threshold of a new intimacy, the desire for which had slipped unnoticed back into my life. As we continued to face each other holding on tightly for reassurance, our emotional scars lay exposed. Vulnerable and newly healed, first by friendship, then trust and finally by love. Love made us infinitely more beautiful in that tender moment.

As we continued to hold each other's hands, the moment expanded like a drop of water, becoming heavier, more rounded, ready to burst. I had imagined many things about a new relationship, but not that it would begin with me bandaged from ankle to thigh, not a classically seductive look. I looked away unable to sustain the intensity of his gaze and began to have doubts, it had been so long since I made love. What if this didn't go well? I can't bear to be touched in a clumsy way, it's a complete turn-off for me. What if I was undesirable? My thoughts accelerated in random waves of uncertainty. Then as if reading them, Mark said "It'll be fine Ellie - it will be fine."

I looked back to his eyes and realised that I loved Mark, partly because he is gentle, self- effacing at times, but underlying those traits, he has a calm strength. His quiet confidence now, stilled my racing thoughts.

We moved, hand in hand, into my room, not led, not following, not infatuated but equal.

Turning to face me, he drew his hands lingeringly from mine and lifted them to move gently through my hair. The carelessly made chignon at the base of my neck released and he combed through it with his slim fingers, tilting my head back to kiss my throat. Never breaking contact his hands travelled over the contours of my body, as he moved them over my hips they slipped under the hem of my jumper and with a deft movement, skinned it away from my body and over my head

Walking backwards to the bed, he neatly scooped me leg and all onto it and I giggled as he tugged my sexless baggy track bottoms off, handling them as if they were the sexiest of silk pyjamas. I watched as he crossed his hands to grasp the hem of his own tee shirt and peel it off overhead. His olive skin glowed honey coloured in the soft light cast from the hall, his lean torso, slender hipped and wide shouldered, was part in shadow, his face completely shaded. I watched the shadows slide over his skin as he bent and moved to remove the rest of his clothes – jealous, as I waited to caress his skin in the way they were now.

I traced every curve of his body as he laid beside me, hands creating a blueprint of his form in my mind, breathing love and desire intermingled, tasting passion, drowning in the depths of this new love. Offering in return the taste of soft-lipped kisses, the warm embrace of my body and tender endearments murmured soft for only him.

That night we moved into a new place of knowing and trusting, our two lonely souls found solace and a new home.

The next morning, I woke to the heavy pressure of Mark's arm across my body and the cocooning warmth of a second body in the bed. A shaft of sunlight streamed in through the window spotlighting both our faces. I watched his chest, brown against my pale skin, rise and fall as he breathed. His face relaxed in sleep, shadowed around the jaw by dark stubble and his mop of curls tousled on the pillow. Waking up beside him felt right. I waited for him to wake and after a few minutes saw his dark lashes flicker and his eyes open sleepily.

"Hey gorgeous, what's your name?" he said lazily.

"Rita!" I flicked back "Is my perfume smelling sweeter - than when you saw me down on the floor?"

He propped up on one elbow, "Oh ho! Very sparky for first thing."

"Been awake longer than you," I laughed leaning over and giving him a kiss. "Now you're awake, I need to pee..."

"Too much information," he complained. "Would you like some tea?"

"Love some." I replied as I tried and miserably failed to walk in some kind of sexy "morning after" kind of a way across to the en-suite, managing only my current dot and carry one, post-op limp. I decided on a careful hand-held shower too, which I'd discovered I could achieve by balancing on the good leg with my bandaged leg hanging outside the cubicle. A bit perilous, but worth it to stand under the shower. I emerged swathed in a soft bathrobe, as Mark in jeans, with bare torso and feet, padded in from the kitchen with two steaming mugs. Placing both on my bedside table, he cupped my face in both hands and said "Beautiful Ellie, you're beautiful and last night was amazing."

"It was for me too."

25.Time together.

The surprises were not over... later at breakfast Mark said "I have something to tell you, I have to go away in a couple of weeks-time."

My heart sank, "Oh, where to?"

"Mauritius, just for a week, a Company I've been consulting for has invited me to speak at a conference for their potential customers."

"Wow, lucky you, the best we Physio's manage is a weekend in Edinburgh or Birmingham."

"They've offered flights for me and a guest. I thought, if you're happy to leave the dogs with Pen for an extra week and the Clinic is safe in Robin's capable hands...you could come with me for a break. You know, be at my beck and call, boost my image as a successful business man..."

I threw the nearest tea towel at his head and as he bent to pick it up said,

"Tell me you aren't teasing...Of course I'd love to come. I'm not sure about the beck and call bit, but I could throw in a personal massage service for you." Then a thought occurred,

"I'll have to check with Walt that he is happy for me to fly, it may be too close to the operation."

"I hadn't thought about that. Your follow-up appointment is tomorrow isn't it? We can confirm then. Have you thought any more about asking Robin to stay on permanently?"

"I haven't had much time; I was rather busy yesterday evening after you mentioned it!

As I ticked off in my mind the people I needed to speak to get the Mauritius trip organised, I also knew there was someone I wanted to speak to about Mark and me - Annie. I didn't need her permission, but I wanted her blessing, as I made this final step away from Brett.

Mark dropped me at Touch just before nine o'clock and drove away as I stood and waved. Everything was quiet when I let myself into the practice, I checked the diary and saw no patients until ten o'clock - good! I needed a few moments to get my head straight, it seemed as though my whole world had just shifted on its axis. I love the energy at Touch and as I let the calm and familiar surroundings of my office enfold me, I began to feel less giddy and more myself. Nine o'clock UK time meant around seven in the evening in Sydney and I may catch Annie. I dialled her number and after a couple of long buzzes her slightly breathless voice said "Annie speaking."

"Annie! It's good to hear your voice, you sound out of breath."

"Ellie! Good to hear you too! I heard the phone ringing as I got to the door, I've just done a run and you know how it is-fumbled the keys, got a bit flustered, thought I'd miss the call."

"I'm glad you picked up, I've got something to tell you."

"Ooooh exciting! Spill the beans, Hun."

"Um, well you know I've spoken about my friend Mark, the one who's converting a barn."

"Yes, I remember, you went to that wedding together before Christmas and you were having kittens about wearing your red Casablanca dress."

"We've become an item, only recently. He's asked me to move in to the barn permanently, not just whilst my leg is healing."

The normal delay on the line, where I heard my words echo like a ghost voice, seemed interminable as I waited for her reaction. "Ellie that's brilliant, I'm so pleased for you. Max will be too. We were only saying the other night we so wanted you to find someone else."

Bless her heart, I felt my throat constrict and a fat tear rolled off my lashes onto the desk.

"Oh Annie, part of me feels guilty to be so happy and making plans for a new life when..."

"I know, I know, but you'll see, it will all work out. This is a good thing. Promise you won't ever lose us though Ellie, just because we were part of a different life with Brett."

"I promise" I said huskily, "You've made me cry you idiot."

"I know, I can hear. You aren't being disloyal if that's what's worrying you. You were with Brett one hundred percent while you could be. He was stolen away Ellie. We still remember you and Brett together too and it's like you're frozen in time happy and smiling in all our photos, but he's been gone a long time and you have to have an open door in your heart and keep living. I think it's time to add new photos to the album now. Send us some of you happy and smiling with Mark and bring him over, we need to vet him."

I will Annie, I'd love to see you both, I miss you."

"Miss you too."

I put the phone down gently.

Noises in the outer office brought me back from Australia. Rose had arrived and I called out greetings, bringing her to my office with a sheath of papers and lots of questions. As we dealt with the matters in hand, Brett and Mark slipped out of my mind. I spoke to Rose about the Mauritius plan to make sure she was comfortable holding the fort. She seemed very eager to get me on that plane and I suspect was secretly relishing the chance to have Robin to herself for another week! I foresaw no problems with my receptionist if Robin agreed to my proposal to stay on.

For the rest of the morning, I worked on figures, stopping only for a chat with two of my long-standing patients - Trish was back for a loosen up and I was very pleased to learn that she was giving Robin a hard time too! Pam's husband Peter was in for a treatment too. I worried about him after Pam died. He seemed rather aloof and distant when she was alive, but clearly, they were much more of a team than seemed obvious, because after her death, he crumpled and aged, losing confidence and looking a little unkempt and faded. However, he was getting better, more like his old self, only more approachable. He had come in to see Robin with a pain in his foot - he'd tripped when he was helping at one of Pam's old charity events. I was glad he was finding a place here in the community after all.

When Robin finished his list, he joined me in the office, perching on the corner of the desk, swinging one leg and somehow exuding the sunshine of his native land from every pore. "Hi how's it going?" I asked.

"Yeah, good thanks Ellie. How about you?"

"Can't wait to get these stitches out and the bandage off " I said "I'm going to book in some appointments with you if you don't mind?"
"Sure, it's going to need some loosening off and work to get your muscles going."
I grimaced - the first few days would be hell trying to bend my knee, we both knew that.
"Robin, I want to put a proposition to you..."
"Well I'm not that kind of guy." he said very straight faced.
I laughed "Oh get over yourself, I am the one woman in town who has not succumbed to your charms."
"You and Trish," he said, ruefully "I'm clearly losing my touch."
"Seriously, I wondered if you might consider staying on here at Touch after I come back. I've built it up in preparation for someone to work with me and we could work out something flexible to let you get away regularly."
"Um - I had sort of imagined working for blocks of time with an agency to get my funds together, then taking off and travelling for blocks of time. I've had another offer too, a guy called Martin rang the Clinic and offered me good money to work with him."
I stared aghast, surely Martin wouldn't get away with poaching Robin from under my nose. "It isn't a good place to work and I could be flexible here, you could easily have long weekends and then take more holiday, so that over the year you worked a sort of 60% post- if that would be enough for you." I stopped just short of begging and realised I had been gabbling. I couldn't bear to think of Robin working for Martin
"Yes, he said you'd say that about working there!"

I handed him a sheet, "Here are the patient numbers over the last couple of years, you can see roughly what you could earn. I need someone to help me, I have a couple of other projects I want to develop outside the practice and can't keep working the hours I have been. You've settled in well here and there is a lot of potential."

"I can see that Ellie, you've built up a great little clinic here and it's a nice town. Don't worry I was teasing, Martin sounded very odd on the phone. He said his latest locum had let him down and left at very short notice."

"Odd? He's horrible Robin and he doesn't look after his patients the way we do either. You could stay on in my cottage if you would like to. I'd need you to cover my mortgage as your rent." I felt a slow blush creep into my cheeks "I am going to stay on at the barn, so will have to rent the cottage out anyway."

He grinned "No wonder you haven't fallen prey to my charm. It's a good offer and I do like it here. Can I think about it and let you know next week?"

"Sure, I wasn't expecting an answer right now, ring me if there is anything else you need to know."

We said goodbye and I watched him leave, hoping against hope he would say yes. I suddenly felt weary and my knee was tight under the bandage. Lack of sleep, some powerful conversations and my world turned upside down, had all taken their toll. I still needed to see Pen though and spend some time with my dogs before going back to the barn, so I rang for a taxi, said my goodbyes to Rose and headed for the farm.

I waved to Pen who was at the kitchen window, working by the sink, as I got out of the taxi. I let myself in through the side door to avoid all the workmen and saw Jeeves and Bird stretched out on the sofa in the kitchen at their ease. They leapt up as I came in and gave me their usual hero's welcome."

"I'd love a walk across the fields." I groaned.

Eyeing my crutches and leg dubiously, Pen said "I don't think that's a good plan, but how about we walk up the driveway towards the Old Farm, the dogs can run on the fields at the top for a bit and we can sit on the seat by the pond and keep them in view."

It was better than nothing, so we set off in cavalcade, dogs delighted to be out as ever, sniffing every blade of grass and tracking scents along the hedge on either side of the drive. As we settled on the slightly rickety, lichen-scarred pond seat and watched the dogs running and playing on the fields. I asked Pen how the work was going in the house.

"Don't ask, I wish we'd never started. I am so sick of dust and men tramping in and out. There always seems to be some kind of hold up. Either someone crucial can't get here or a pipe is the wrong size or something. What about you? What have you been up to today, apart from falling deeper in love with the adorable Mark?"

"Well..." I explained about Marks invitation to stay on at the barn and the other invitation to Mauritius and his idea of asking of Robin to stay on."

"Ellie! I only saw you yesterday morning! Your whole life seems to have changed; you've had quite a day..."

"Tell me about it" I complained "I don't quite know what is happening, but I feel like someone turned the handle and a whole set of events just started to cascade - it's like real life Mousetrap."

"Perhaps it was all just meant to be. I'm so jealous about the trip to Mauritius, just don't you dare go off and get married in secret whilst you're over there, I would never forgive you. I want the whole works, bridesmaid's dress, dogs with decorated collars carrying the train of your gown etc."

"Married? Steady on, I think you read too many romantic novels. I'm not getting married and who would be mad enough to have Setters carrying the train of their dress, especially Setters trained by us! What a hoot! I'd be in tatters in seconds, not to mention the ensuing riot in the assembled company as paw prints and slobber got distributed without fear of favour onto expensive outfits."

We started to laugh.

"Goodness, can you imagine the carnage," she snorted "Be worth it for the video."

"Yes well," I said wiping my eyes, "Good job there's no wedding on the horizon."

We whistled the dogs in and set off towards Pen's house again.

Pen dropped me back to the barn and I let myself in feeling I'd accomplished a lot today. As I swung my leg up onto the bed to give it ten minutes respite, I had every intention of processing it all and planning for the next couple of weeks, then getting dinner underway for the two of us. Instead of which sleep overcame me and I knew nothing more until Mark woke me for the dinner that he'd prepared instead.

As I arrived for my appointment the next morning, Walt greeted me cheerfully, "Ellie, come on in." "How has it been?"

"Truthfully, a bit grim to start with, but the last few days have been better, I'm getting less pain now."

"Let's have a look, shall we? Can you bend it, It'll be stiff to start with."

Stiff! That was the understatement of the year, I managed to bend to nearly a right angle and then the front of my knee felt like it was going to burst.

"That's not bad, look I'm sure you've got a Physio friend, or, you can come to the department here, but you'll need some treatment.

"I'm going to have some appointments with Robin the Physio who is covering me at the Clinic. Is it alright for me to walk my dogs again? I can walk them off lead."

"Well, I'd like you to have a stick or a crutch when you're on rough ground for another couple of weeks and take someone with you to be on the safe side"

"Next question, I've got the opportunity to go to Mauritius in two weeks-time, can I go or is it too close to the general anaesthetic?" I held my breath, I know the minimum time before flying can be as short as a few days but sometimes the surgeon prefers longer...

"That should be fine, wear compression socks and make sure you move around regularly during the flight. What takes you to Mauritius?"

"My boyfriend has asked me to go to help him at a conference, he's giving a lecture, but it's mainly a holiday for me." I felt a little zing of joy as I used the 'boyfriend' word it still felt new and good.

"Lucky you, enjoy! Just don't overdo it, the worst thing you can do is make the knee aggravated and swollen, it can be a nightmare to settle down - but you know that."

"I was thinking I could phase back into work after I've been away as well?"

"You do mainly outpatients, don't you?"

I nodded.

"That should be fine then, just stay off any heavy lifting or twisting until the six-week mark. Get in contact when you're back anyway Ellie, I was hoping we could have a chat about my knee patients who've had the same surgery as you. I'd like to refer them to you in future, as you've had experience of the procedure."

"Brilliant, that would be amazing, I'd like to get involved with that. Thank you for looking after me and fitting me in so quickly."

"My pleasure Ellie, look after yourself and no more accidents." He shook my hand and ushered me out, by the look of the waiting area he had a busy clinic to get through, getting a steady stream of referrals from here would be good for Touch.

I couldn't wait to tell Mark the good news...Mauritius on the horizon and a new arrangement that would bring in a lot of work to Touch, all in one day. I felt some of the weight of worry lifting off my shoulders.

26.Mauritius.

With Mauritius as my goal, I phoned Rose and booked in to see Robin the following day to get my therapy started.

Mark got home about six and looked tired from the driving, but his face lit up when he saw me without crutches and said "Mauritius?"

I mimicked Meg Ryan's scene in When Harry met Sally. "Yes, yes, yes!"

"We're going to have fun. That's brilliant news."

The two weeks before we left, flew past in a haze of activity. Physio appointments every other day, during which Robin did not spare me. He was good at his job and painfully my knee started to bend further, my leg got stronger and I felt confident that it wouldn't let me down.

Rose called me into my office after my second appointment and shut the door looking cock-a-hoop. She had been visiting a friend who lived close to Martin's practice and had heard a juicy piece of gossip.

"Guess what? Martin is in trouble apparently. A notice announcing that he is no longer working in the Practice, and it's now being run by Jana has been posted in the local paper."

"Oh, wow! I know this isn't very nice of me, but if she has
"Apparently, rumour has it that he's been having an affair with the young physio who had replaced you."
"That doesn't surprise me, he thinks he's God's gift to women."
"Yes, but it turns out that the money for the premises and most of the start-up capital was from Jana's parents. None of it was actually his."
"Brilliant! She's finally stood up to him, good for her. Well it couldn't have happened to a nicer bloke - not!"
I hoped Jana made a go of it and that her heart wasn't broken. I'd call her when we got back from holiday to wish her luck.
Back at home, the dogs made the transition to the barn without question and we met Pen most days for our walk with her two. Much to Mark's disapproval, because I wasn't supposed to take them out alone, I did sneak off on my own to walk them, a couple of times, I need space sometimes.
He was very busy tying up loose ends with various clients before we went away and I didn't see a great deal of him, other than catching up in the evenings. We had a comfortable rhythm and it felt good sitting together on the sofa, his arm round my shoulders or me sitting sideways with my legs across his lap.
Departure day dawned and I followed Mark into the Business Class lounge at Heathrow. I was used to both of us in casual clothes, apart from the black tie do before Christmas. I'd seen him in the occasional suit, briefly, as he flew through the door on his way to meet clients, but today travelling with him for work, he seemed a lot more grown up and assured. He looked good in his charcoal grey suit, with a white shirt and a pale grey tie, curls tamed with gel. I had

chosen to travel in a pair of navy palazzo pants and a cream blazer with navy trim, over a camisole. Flat shoes were the order of the day for me, because my knee was still a bit painful, who am I trying to kid, I'm nearly always in flats. I desperately hoped I looked like Julia Roberts in Pretty Woman, although with slight limp and woeful lack of inches somehow doubted it. I felt a bit out of place but reminded myself that I met and chatted to people all day, this would be no different.

"You look very professional," I confided, as we accepted a glass of champagne.

"Did you think I wouldn't?" He cocked an eyebrow at me teasing.

"I don't know really, I'm just used to Mark on the farm, I've never imagined you at work."

"Beware! I am very demanding."

"Shame I don't wear glasses, I could disarm you as I remove them, let my hair down with a swish and bowl you over!"

"Done." He said. "Already done - bowled over and out. I can return the compliment too, you look very smart yourself."

"Beats joggers and baggy tee shirts...I do possess some smart clothes for when I lecture, I just don't wear them very often. I've packed all my beach gear too, so I shall make you jealous if you have to work too hard"

"My talk is on the second day and after that I'll have to be around for some of the break-out groups but other than that time is my own"

"Sounds perfect."

People say they don't enjoy flights much, but I do, it's such a luxury to have twelve hours to do nothing but read, write, watch movies and snooze. Meals and drinks brought to you and no control or responsibility for anything - bliss on a stick. Business class made it even more of a treat and I settled in to thoroughly enjoy myself. Mark was tired and fell asleep before me, I watched him sleep for a while, the thin airline blanket folding loosely about his slender body, one slim hand resting across the folds and his breathing rhythmic, chest rising and falling under the cover. He looked peaceful and vulnerable lying there and I felt a fierce surge of protective love for him.

The last of the Mauritian summer heat made itself apparent immediately we left the plane and was quite a shock after our fresh spring temperatures at home. A driver was waiting for us with a placard "Mr M Roxbury" and we were ushered to our car like royalty. The beautiful Baie aux Tortues where we were staying, about an hour from the airport. Jean our driver pointed out the sights as we drove and I was mesmerised by the lush greenness, the curious shapes of the volcanic hills and perilous looking rock formations. It was the sea that finally took my breath away as we walked into our suite. It lay beyond the coconut palms and the beach, glinting azure in the sun and lapping gently at the shore. The great waves of the Indian Ocean visible in the distance, beyond the mouth of the calm bay.

I pushed open the balcony door and leant on the wall gazing out. Mark slung his jacket onto the bed loosened his tie and top button, then came to join me wrapping his arms around me from behind

"It's beautiful." I half whispered "Thank you for this."

"I'm glad you're here Ellie, I love you."

"I love you too."

I kissed him and took his hand drawing him back inside. He looked impossibly sexy in a tired, travel worn way, his eyes alight with mischief and desire. An unexpected sharp tug on my hand pulled me suddenly into him and he bent his head to kiss me long and slow, ridding my mind of every thought and making my body languorous as I moulded to him. He took the hand he was still holding and bent it back as if to kiss the pulse point inside my wrist then instead, nipped the pads of each finger, lighting small fires that flamed through me, fanned as he blew softly along the tender skin inside my arm. Clothes were shed like falling leaves and left unheeded on the floor. I felt the cool cotton of the crisp sheets and the warmth of Mark as we claimed the bed and abandoned my body to sensation alone.

"Wake up sleepy," I trailed my fingers over his chest and shook him gently with the flat of my hand "We have a cocktail reception in an hour."

"Oh no," he groaned "really?"

"Yes indeed, I've been reading the itinerary and that's what it says..."

"Didn't you sleep?"

"Not really, I sneaked down to the beach and had a dip, the water looked and is gorgeous, then I've been on the balcony reading the conference programme."

"Smart casual tonight."

"It'll be interminable," he grumbled "everyone being over friendly and the inevitable idiot who drinks too much."

"People in glass houses..." I laughed thinking back to the wedding reception "Come on don't be grumpy, it'll be fun, anyway I want to see you at work."

Still looking owlish, he slouched off to the shower and emerged more awake and resigned to his fate. We dressed and walked down the wide tiled steps and through the stunning park to the balcony bar above the restaurant. A young musician played jazz on a white grand piano and the hum of a hundred different conversations filled the room.

I enjoyed myself chatting to all sorts of people and watched Mark clearly confident and at ease, he'd obviously done all this before.

As the evening ended, we said goodnight to everyone and walked back to our room via the beach. Sandals swinging from one hand and holding Marks hand with the other, I enjoyed the gritty feel of the sand under my bare feet. The night breeze blew cool on my skin and the calm sea appeared transformed by moonlight into a magical lagoon of liquid silver. I felt like the cat who got the cream.

Lazy breakfast, beanbag on the beach, books, swimming, exercises, cocktails and dinner became my punishing routine for the week. Mark joined me when he could and it was good to see him relax as his tan deepened and the dark circles under his eyes disappeared. Out of our usual environment, we had uninterrupted time to talk and as the week sped by, I felt more and more comfortable with our decision to move in together, it seemed less impetuous and more a natural extension of our deepening relationship.

On the evening before we left, Mark had a panel session followed by a formal dinner, which I elected not to attend, preferring to rest my knee before the next day's journey. I sat on the balcony in the balmy night and rocked gently in the hammock chair, lulled and soothed into a dreamy muse. The palm trees seemed to whisper to each other, but I could overhear their secrets as I rocked gently to and fro. The steady pulse of the sea rolled, calmly hypnotic and I felt blessed to once more love and feel loved.

27. The Fete.

Our journey home was uneventful, but the relaxed pace of the island didn't last. We had little opportunity to linger with nostalgic thoughts about Mauritius. The conference generated several excellent leads for Mark and he was extremely busy. Some days, we only managed a flying kiss in the morning, toast in hand and a quick chat over a reheated dinner last thing at night. My phased return to the Clinic was a bit less gradual than I had intended too, but I loved being back in the swing of things and there was indeed enough work for both Robin and me.

He came to see me about a week after my return.

"Ellie, I've been thinking about your proposal and I would like to give it a go."

"Robin that's brilliant news."

"I'd like to take up your offer of renting the cottage for the time being too, if you're still thinking along those lines, I like it there, it suits me."

I had a brief moment of panic...was I ready to let go of my safe place even temporarily? It suited me too. Then I thought how happy Mark and I were at the barn. Brett came to mind, he always encouraged me to move forward. He'd be giving me one of his irritating Casablanca quotes "You'll regret it, not today, not tomorrow, but soon." And he'd be right, it was time I moved forward into my new life.

"Yes of course, that would be great, I will come and take the rest of my clothes out and clear my clutter, would you like to keep the furniture as it is, or is there anything you want to move?"

"No, it's fine as is."

I punched the air in my imagination, I really liked working with Robin it was great to have someone to bounce ideas off and a second pair of eyes to help with tricky patients, after a long patch working alone. I couldn't wait to tell Mark.

I finished off my notes, leant back in the office chair and yawned, time to head for home. Voices sounded in reception and then came a knock on the door.

"Come in."

"Sorry to disturb you," said Rose, "some lads are here from the Rugby Club to see you."

"This looks ominous," I said as I saw the motley crew of rugby players in reception. "What can I do for you?"

"Hi Ellie," said Paul, the current first team captain, grasping my relatively small hand in his huge mitt and giving it a friendly crush. "We're doing a community day on the 21st July to raise money for the Club and for the local Hospice. Would you support it by having a stall and perhaps do a demonstration? We'd like to make it a village fete during the day, with a live band and a dance in the evening."

"Sounds like a great idea" I replied checking in my diary. "Yes, put Touch down for a stall, we can plan something interesting. I can contact the Gym Club if you like and see if they'll do a demonstration too.

"Amazing Ellie - Thanks."

The day of the fete dawned a little overcast, but as the morning wore on the clouds cleared and it looked set fair for a sunny afternoon much to everyone's relief. I had roped-in as many friends and family as I could to help. Mark, Dom, Angus and the rugby lads worked like trojans all morning setting up gazebo's and tables, then ferrying back and forwards to collect equipment. Stallholders decorated their tables, floats were distributed, my Dad was up a ladder nailing up the bunting strung around the club and Mum made everlasting cups of tea in the clubhouse kitchen, flushed with the heat and her delight at pitching in.

"She's great your Mum," Paul said, emerging from the clubhouse with a steaming mug and a sandwich.

"Yep, she loves an excuse to feed people."

We were just about ready, as people started to arrive for the two o'clock start.

Pen's cake stall looked amazing, crisp white tablecloths set off the rich colours of ginger cake, Victoria sponge, fruit loaf and my favourite lemon drizzle, all displayed on pretty china plates. As a tribute to Pam, Pen had asked Peter if she could use her recipes. Peter had not only given the recipes, but had paid to have a recipe book simply bound, with a dedication to Pam: "There is much comfort in good cake." He volunteered to help Pen on the stall and it was good to see him selling the cakes. So many people had a story about Pam and her cakes, he could not fail to realise how much she had been loved.

Mark's Mum helped Angus set up his games stall next door to them and was a dab hand at the one where you guide the loop along the wire without making contact or setting off the buzzer. She made it look easy, laughing delightedly, which encouraged people to give it a go and I noticed her and Peter chatting together on and off during the afternoon.

"Mark didn't tell me there would be such handsome men to flirt with," she whispered to me as she came to look at the clinic's stall, but as she was having her posture checked by Robin at the time, I wasn't entirely sure who she meant.

Our stall was busy all afternoon, Rose and Jen chatting to people and handing out leaflets whilst they waited for Robin or me to check out their posture. We showed them the shape of their spine by moulding their backs with an artist's curve and chatted about corrections. Lots of folk tried out the ergonomic office chair and looked at how to set up their work stations too. I was amazed how many ex-patients and others we knew came by to say hello and felt touched that the clinic had indeed become part of this community as I'd hoped it would be. The only time we stopped, was for the stretching and Gym Ball demonstrations which were executed by Vale with her usual grace, Mark under sufferance and with comic inaccuracy by Dominic, who could not be said to be supple. However, he encouraged people to come and have a go themselves by saying "You can't be worse than me!"

Luke came by the stall after their amazing tumbling display. "Bravo Luke," I said "breath-taking! I see your foot is all good again."

"Yes, I'm back into training properly and I have some great news, I've been invited to train with the England squad for a weekend as a guest, I can't wait."

"That's brilliant, congratulations. Just don't injure anything else before you go."

As I watched him walk away towards the other gymnasts, I felt proud, I was sure he was on his way to well-deserved success.

By the time the afternoon fete was over and we had taken the equipment back to the practice, the band were tuning up for the evening dance. We were all ravenous and thirsty, so took no persuading to partake of succulent hog roast in crusty rolls with crackling and sharp apple sauce. We pulled tables together, Peter joined the party, and Dom and Mark brought back a jug of local beer and some cider which hit the spot perfectly.

"Cheers everyone and thank you for all your hard work," I said raising my glass, "good day!" I sighed with satisfaction as the first mouthful of cider slaked my thirst.

"Good day!" They toasted back.

As the evening wore on and the shadows lengthened, green bushes became dark silhouettes and the wide Essex sky turned a fiery red. I snuggled into Marks jumper, the long arms covering my hands and leant back against him watching the band. Pen and Angus were near the bar chatting to their young farmer friends. Vale and Dom were in the middle dancing. As I watched, I saw him gently ruffle her hair as she looked up smiling and I caught a look that passed between them. "Mark do you think those two will make a go of it?"

"They only met today," he replied and I realised he was looking at Peter and Alessandra also dancing together.

"No, Dom and Vale," I said "although would you mind? They seem to have hit it off."

"I wouldn't mind at all, it'd be good for both of them, Mum gets lonely and I'm sure Peter does too. And yes, Dom is completely smitten, I've never known him like this with anyone before."

"I hope so, I like Vale."

I could see Robin chatting to a slender blonde at the bar too, and when she turned I realised it was Louise. She was laughing at something he had said and looked younger, relaxed and more casual in her jeans and jumper. I was glad to see her having fun.

It came to me that I felt contented, so different from the girl who had come to Essex, her life in tatters, looking for a place to hide. Slowly, slowly this community with all its characters had become home, Touch my place of salvation, Pen and Angus, Vale and Dom, more like family.

I felt Mark kiss the top of my head. "A penny for them."

"I'm so happy Mark, there is nowhere I would rather be."

"I love you Ellie Rose."

"I love you too."

As night fell, people became moving shadows in the shifting lights of the stage. A crescent moon lazed on its back in the inky sky. Still in the darkness, I felt at peace with the arms of my love around me and at peace within my soul.

Married with two grown-up sons and a clan of Gordon Setter dogs, ANGELA CAIRNS is a Physiotherapist and Acupuncturist. She directs two multidisciplinary Clinics, lectures in Physiotherapy and broadcast for twenty years with BBC Essex as their Sound Advice Physiotherapist. Writing has always been part of her life; PlayPauseUnwind 1 & 2 are collections of relaxation stories with original soundtracks and she is a contributor to short story anthology – "Paths Made by Walking." Touch and its cast of characters are from her imagination, but their authenticity comes from her passion for people and many years' experience working with them.

www.angelacairnsauthor.co.uk
Fb @angelacairnsauthor
Instagram angelacairnsauthor

Printed in Poland
by Amazon Fulfillment
Poland Sp. z o.o., Wrocław